P9-EGM-045

SPECTRUM

Math

Grade 3

Published by Spectrum
an imprint of Carson-Dellosa Publishing
Greensboro, NC

Spectrum
An imprint of Carson-Dellosa Publishing LLC
P.O. Box 35665
Greensboro, NC 27425 USA

© 2007 Carson-Dellosa Publishing LLC. Except as permitted under the United States Copyright Act, no part of this publication may be reproduced, stored, or distributed in any form or by any means (mechanically, electronically, recording, etc.) without the prior written consent of Carson-Dellosa Publishing LLC. Spectrum is an imprint of Carson-Dellosa Publishing LLC.

Printed in the USA • All rights reserved.

ISBN 0-7696-3693-4

-252117811

NAME ________________

CHAPTER 1 PRETEST

Check What You Know

Adding and Subtracting 1- and 2-Digit Numbers (with renaming)

Add.

	a	b	c	d	e
1.	23 + 19	17 + 5	37 + 42	11 + 75	81 + 9
2.	16 + 3	83 + 11	43 + 14	22 + 59	64 + 6
3.	30 + 23	17 + 25	19 + 36	18 + 25	93 + 2
4.	13 + 86	75 + 3 + 16	13 + 33 + 7	40 + 51 + 2	15 + 27 + 46

Subtract.

	a	b	c	d	e
5.	90 − 10	16 − 9	23 − 18	27 − 7	19 − 11
6.	57 − 16	84 − 23	16 − 11	25 − 5	62 − 19
7.	97 − 58	46 − 23	81 − 27	48 − 13	74 − 9
8.	32 − 24	73 − 12	65 − 30	70 − 20	23 − 8

NAME ____________________

Check What You Know

SHOW YOUR WORK

Adding and Subtracting 1- and 2-Digit Numbers (with renaming)

Solve each problem.

9. The florist has 63 roses and carnations. If she has 27 roses, how many carnations does she have?

The florist has ________ roses and carnations.

She has ________ roses.

The florist has ________ carnations.

10. Bly has 43 pennies, 13 dimes, and 16 nickels. How many coins does she have in all?

Bly has ________ pennies.

She has ________ dimes.

She has ________ nickels.

Bly has ________ coins in all.

11. There are 36 students in Cleveland's class this year. If 22 are girls, how many boys are in Cleveland's class?

There are ________ students in Cleveland's class.

There are ________ girls in his class.

There are ________ boys in his class.

12. The store has 53 cases of apples and oranges in the storeroom. If there are 28 cases of apples, how many cases of oranges are there in the storeroom?

There are ________ cases of oranges in the storeroom.

9.

10.

11.

12.

NAME ______________________

Lesson 1.1 Adding through 18

addend 3 → Find the **3**-row.
addend + 8 → Find the **8**-column.
sum 11 ← The sum is named where the 3-row and the 8-column meet.

8-column
Addend

3-row

Addend

+	0	1	2	3	4	5	6	7	8	9
0	0	1	2	3	4	5	6	7	8	9
1	1	2	3	4	5	6	7	8	9	10
2	2	3	4	5	6	7	8	9	10	11
3	3	4	5	6	7	8	9	10	11	12
4	4	5	6	7	8	9	10	11	12	13
5	5	6	7	8	9	10	11	12	13	14
6	6	7	8	9	10	11	12	13	14	15
7	7	8	9	10	11	12	13	14	15	16
8	8	9	10	11	12	13	14	15	16	17
9	9	10	11	12	13	14	15	16	17	18

Add.

	a	b	c	d	e	f
1.	2 + 3	7 + 9	2 + 5	1 + 7	0 + 3	9 + 5
2.	7 + 2	3 + 3	9 + 0	6 + 5	0 + 7	8 + 5
3.	4 + 3	2 + 9	7 + 7	5 + 6	5 + 9	0 + 6
4.	0 + 0	8 + 3	8 + 6	6 + 1	5 + 3	4 + 8
5.	5 + 2	3 + 1	2 + 4	8 + 2	8 + 8	3 + 6
6.	4 + 6	5 + 0	3 + 7	6 + 9	9 + 9	5 + 7

NAME ______________________________

Lesson 1.2 Subtracting through 18

minuend 12 → Find the **12** in
subtrahend − 7 → the **7**-column.
difference 5 ← The difference is the number at the end of the row.

7-column

−	0	1	2	3	4	5	6	7	8	9
0	0	1	2	3	4	5	6	7	8	9
1	1	2	3	4	5	6	7	8	9	10
2	2	3	4	5	6	7	8	9	10	11
3	3	4	5	6	7	8	9	10	11	12
4	4	5	6	7	8	9	10	11	12	13
5	5	6	7	8	9	10	11	12	13	14
6	6	7	8	9	10	11	12	13	14	15
7	7	8	9	10	11	12	13	14	15	16
8	8	9	10	11	12	13	14	15	16	17
9	9	10	11	12	13	14	15	16	17	18

Subtract.

	a	b	c	d	e	f
1.	7 − 2	6 − 0	5 − 4	11 − 6	16 − 9	13 − 8
2.	6 − 3	9 − 6	5 − 2	8 − 0	18 − 9	9 − 7
3.	7 − 2	3 − 0	8 − 2	7 − 4	10 − 3	9 − 2
4.	4 − 0	3 − 2	9 − 3	13 − 5	13 − 8	8 − 4
5.	12 − 5	6 − 4	1 − 0	12 − 3	10 − 6	11 − 5
6.	3 − 1	4 − 3	9 − 1	5 − 1	8 − 7	14 − 8

NAME ____________________

Lesson 1.3 Adding 2-Digit Numbers (no renaming)

First, add the ones. Then, add the tens.

43	43	43	addend
+22	+22	+22	addend
	5	65	sum

22	addend
+16	addend
38	sum

First, add the ones.
Then, add the tens.

Add.

	a	b	c	d	e	f
1.	23 + 16 = 39	11 + 22 = 33	20 + 10 = 30	16 + 12 = 28	73 + 15 = 88	63 + 13 = 76
2.	10 + 17 = 27	18 + 30 = 48	13 + 14 = 27	32 + 51 = 83	81 + 11 = 92	34 + 21 = 55
3.	14 + 12 = 26	34 + 13 = 47	41 + 18 = 59	30 + 50 = 80	27 + 50 = 77	22 + 22 = 44
4.	18 + 41 = 59	13 + 42 = 55	12 + 44 = 56	31 + 17 = 48	27 + 42 = 69	31 + 38 = 64
5.	13 + 14 = 27	15 + 43 = 58	23 + 42 = 65	22 + 71 = 93	37 + 60 = 97	35 + 23 = 58
6.	10 + 43 = 53	73 + 20 = 93	86 + 13 = 99	52 + 13 = 65	42 + 26 = 68	32 + 45 = 77

NAME ______________________________

Lesson 1.4 Subtracting 2-Digit Numbers (no renaming)

First, subtract the ones. Then, subtract the tens.

$\begin{array}{r} 36 \\ -23 \\ \hline \end{array}$	$\begin{array}{r} 36 \\ -23 \\ \hline 3 \end{array}$	$\begin{array}{r} 36 \\ -23 \\ \hline 13 \end{array}$	minuend subtrahend difference

Subtract.

	a	b	c	d	e	f
1.	$23 - 12$	$86 - 22$	$93 - 71$	$30 - 10$	$92 - 11$	$48 - 16$
2.	$62 - 10$	$83 - 13$	$65 - 44$	$54 - 12$	$37 - 25$	$88 - 32$
3.	$86 - 45$	$92 - 70$	$89 - 62$	$75 - 62$	$88 - 44$	$90 - 60$
4.	$82 - 41$	$57 - 36$	$35 - 23$	$65 - 43$	$81 - 60$	$42 - 30$
5.	$60 - 30$	$46 - 25$	$92 - 81$	$86 - 32$	$57 - 36$	$29 - 13$
6.	$25 - 15$	$28 - 12$	$36 - 13$	$46 - 15$	$75 - 14$	$64 - 23$

NAME ____________________

Lesson 1.5 Adding 2-Digit Numbers (with renaming)

	Add the ones. Rename 12 as 10 + 2.		Add the tens.	
37 + 25	7 + 5 = 12 or 10 + 2	$\overset{1}{3}7$ + 25 = 2	$\overset{1}{3}7$ + 25 = 62	addend, addend, sum

Add.

	a	b	c	d	e	f
1.	23 + 18	76 + 15	13 + 77	36 + 16	19 + 62	29 + 19
2.	27 + 36	52 + 39	36 + 28	30 + 50	56 + 27	59 + 13
3.	54 + 27	53 + 28	28 + 17	13 + 19	39 + 17	56 + 14
4.	62 + 19	27 + 18	26 + 55	18 + 13	72 + 18	37 + 17
5.	23 + 57	29 + 16	25 + 16	38 + 14	26 + 28	76 + 15
6.	29 + 17	34 + 27	43 + 27	25 + 26	48 + 12	45 + 46

NAME ______________________

Lesson 1.6 Subtracting 2-Digit Numbers (with renaming)

	Subtract the ones. Rename 52 as "4 tens and 12 ones."	Subtract the ones.	Subtract the tens.	
52	$\overset{4\,12}{\cancel{5}\cancel{2}}$	$\overset{4\,12}{\cancel{5}\cancel{2}}$	$\overset{4\,12}{\cancel{5}\cancel{2}}$	minuend
−19	−19	−19	−19	subtrahend
		3	33	difference

Subtract.

	a	b	c	d	e	f
1.	30 − 22	22 − 19	53 − 28	41 − 27	92 − 56	86 − 27
2.	83 − 66	62 − 56	51 − 17	34 − 15	46 − 29	57 − 38
3.	72 − 37	82 − 67	64 − 18	86 − 57	41 − 16	53 − 29
4.	24 − 17	60 − 20	86 − 27	93 − 26	52 − 17	47 − 28
5.	86 − 38	45 − 18	42 − 19	96 − 39	63 − 27	87 − 68
6.	53 − 17	92 − 45	86 − 18	72 − 17	63 − 45	52 − 13

NAME ____________________

Lesson 1.7 Adding Three Numbers

Add the ones. Add the tens.

```
  23      3 \
  47      7 /   10              ¹              ¹
 +16     +6    + 6            23            23   addend
                              47            47   addend
               16 or 10 + 6  +16           +16   addend
                                6           86   sum
```

Add.

	a	b	c	d	e	f
1.	13 + 26 + 45	27 + 29 + 56	16 + 23 + 25	27 + 7 + 34	16 + 13 + 29	10 + 30 + 50
2.	22 + 31 + 45	19 + 21 + 32	29 + 16 + 15	13 + 15 + 25	42 + 21 + 8	26 + 23 + 35
3.	11 + 30 + 42	27 + 16 + 9	4 + 7 + 8	34 + 16 + 41	16 + 23 + 35	29 + 31 + 25
4.	82 + 5 + 9	33 + 47 + 12	86 + 5 + 2	18 + 32 + 16	46 + 29 + 16	53 + 21 + 15
5.	66 + 21 + 8	47 + 13 + 8	22 + 41 + 28	23 + 15 + 17	18 + 16 + 24	23 + 35 + 17

NAME ____________________

Lesson 1.8 Addition and Subtraction Practice

Add or subtract.

	a	b	c	d	e	f
1.	23 − 10	76 + 21	82 − 19	16 + 7 + 13	16 + 35	76 − 30
2.	20 + 50	30 − 13	16 + 13 + 23	76 − 43	87 − 45	92 − 79
3.	26 + 58	96 − 17	72 + 3	79 + 8	16 − 8	18 + 12 + 42
4.	86 − 19	77 + 16	43 − 29	16 + 7	82 − 42	86 − 39
5.	57 − 43	9 + 9	0 + 30	41 − 22	18 + 42 + 13	18 + 53
6.	81 − 79	27 + 34	86 + 13	92 − 36	37 − 24	86 + 5

NAME ____________________

Lesson 1.9 Problem Solving

SHOW YOUR WORK

Solve each problem.

1. Philip has 52 marbles. His friend, Edgar, has 39 marbles. How many marbles do they have in all?

Philip has __52__ marbles.

Edgar has __39__ marbles.

They have __91__ marbles in all.

2. Susan has 3 cats. George has 23 fish. Maria has 2 birds. How many pets do they have together?

Susan has __3__ cats.

George has __23__ fish.

Maria has __2__ birds.

Together they have __28__ pets.

3. Mr. Williams' third-grade class has 27 students. Mrs. Nakagawa's third-grade class has 31 students. How many third-grade students are there?

Mr. Williams has __27__ students.

Mrs. Nakagawa has __31__ students.

Together, there are __58__ students.

4. There are 36 adults and 17 children at the movie theater. How many people are at the movie theater?

There are __43__ people at the movie theater.

5. Kyle has 77 baseball trading cards. If Omar gives Kyle 13 baseball trading cards, how many trading cards will Kyle have?

Kyle will have __90__ baseball trading cards.

1. 52 + 39 = 91

2. 3 + 23 + 2 = 28

3. 27 + 31 = 58

4. 36 + 17 = 43

5. 77 + 13 = 90

NAME ____________________

Lesson 1.10 Problem Solving

SHOW YOUR WORK

Solve each problem.

1. Mrs. Lopez has 32 rose bushes in her garden. If 14 are not blooming, how many are blooming?

Mrs. Lopez has ________ rose bushes in her garden.

There are ________ bushes that are not blooming.

There are ________ bushes that are blooming.

2. Tamika has 15 cousins. If 11 of her cousins are girls, how many of her cousins are boys?

Tamika has ________ cousins.

She has ________ cousins who are girls.

Tamika has ________ cousins who are boys.

3. There are 76 seats on the plane. There are 62 passengers on the plane. How many empty seats are on the plane?

There are ________ seats on the plane.

There are ________ passengers.

There are ________ empty seats on the plane.

4. There are 56 books on the bookshelf. If 39 are not mystery books, how many are mystery books?

There are ________ mystery books on the bookshelf.

5. My book has 38 pages in it. If there are 12 pages that have pictures, how many pages do not have pictures?

There are ________ pages in the book that do not have pictures.

1.

2.

3.

4.

5.

NAME ______________________

Check What You Learned

Adding and Subtracting 1- and 2-Digit Numbers (with renaming)

Add.

	a	b	c	d	e	f
1.	23 + 47	17 + 22	18 + 53	6 + 27	30 + 50	27 + 0
2.	86 + 12	63 + 29	13 + 37	47 + 23	19 + 29	63 + 21
3.	25 + 35	5 + 31	20 + 0	49 + 26	33 + 44	46 + 53
4.	86 + 5	75 + 6	13 + 12 + 23	63 + 19 + 8	11 + 22 + 33	16 + 32 + 11

Subtract.

	a	b	c	d	e	f
5.	93 − 5	76 − 13	82 − 45	67 − 41	14 − 12	63 − 0
6.	87 − 19	28 − 13	65 − 42	57 − 35	63 − 14	39 − 25
7.	46 − 23	80 − 20	65 − 9	92 − 45	99 − 35	86 − 19
8.	53 − 45	39 − 23	86 − 14	92 − 47	85 − 45	62 − 37

CHAPTER 1 POSTTEST

NAME ______________________

Check What You Learned

SHOW YOUR WORK

Adding and Subtracting 1- and 2-Digit Numbers (with renaming)

Solve each problem.

9. At an air show there were 32 airplanes in the sky. If 15 airplanes landed, how many were still in the sky?

There were ________ airplanes still in the sky.

10. One bag of rocks weighs 15 pounds. Another bag of rocks weighs 23 pounds. How much do both bags of rocks weigh?

Together, the bags of rocks weigh ________ pounds.

11. There were 46 people at the train station. 27 people got on the train. How many people are still at the train station?

There are ________ people still at the train station.

12. Sally has 32 cupcakes. She gave cupcakes to 16 people. How many cupcakes does she have left?

Sally has ________ cupcakes left.

13. The car dealer had 17 model cars. Yesterday, he sold 9 of the model cars. How many model cars does he have left?

The car dealer has ________ model cars left.

14. Beatrix had invited 26 people to her party. Only 9 people could not come to the party. How many people will be at Beatrix's party?

There will be ________ people at Beatrix's party.

NAME ________________

Check What You Know

Numeration through 100,000

Show the value of 5 in each number.

	a	b	c	d
1.	325	395,061	4,500	49,705
2.	5,439	542,960	437,590	753

What digit is in the place named?

	a	b	c	d
3.	5,764 tens	432 ones	5,940 thousands	631 hundreds
4.	459,643 ten thousands	93,046 hundreds	9,764 tens	403,000 hundred thousands

Write each number in expanded form.

	a	b	c	d
5.	596	40,321	170,018	90,431
6.	73	987	5,041	803,731

NAME ____________________

Check What You Know

Numeration through 100,000

Compare each pair of numbers. Write $<$, $>$, or $=$.

	a	b	c	d
7.	30 ____ 32	9 ____ 10	171 ____ 1,710	596 ____ 593
8.	43 ____ 27	30 ____ 30	16 ____ 13	960 ____ 431

Circle the greatest number.

	a	b	c	d
9.	32 14 96	17 21 17	191 25 460	43 57 21

Round each number to the place named.

	a	b	c	d
10.	543 tens ____	867 hundreds ____	479 tens ____	962 tens ____
11.	5,678 thousands ____	9,654 tens ____	7,432 hundreds ____	1,605 tens ____

SHOW YOUR WORK

Solve each problem.

12. Write the greatest number that you can write using the digits 5, 9, 8, and 1.

The largest number is ____________.

13. Write the smallest number that you can write using the digits 7, 3, 2, and 2.

The smallest number is ____________.

14. If Susana has 5 dimes and Rick has 13 dimes, who has the most dimes?

____________ has the most dimes.

12.

13.

14.

NAME ______________________

Lesson 2.1 Understanding Place Value (to hundreds)

Use this chart to help you tell the value of each digit.

Hundreds	Tens	Ones
5	7	2
The value of 5 is 5 hundreds or 500.	The value of 7 is 7 tens or 70.	The value of 2 is 2 ones or 2.

The expanded form of a number is written as a sum showing the place values.

The expanded form of 572 is 500 + 70 + 2.

Show the value of 3 in each number.

	a	b	c	d
1.	324 300	135 30	36 30	513 3

Name the value of the digit in the place named.

	a	b	c	d
2.	231 hundreds 200	63 ones 3	725 tens 20	123 tens 2
3.	691 tens 9	192 ones 2	23 tens 2	392 hundreds 3

Write each number in expanded form.

	a	b	c	d
4.	563 500+60+3	92 90+2	861 800+60+1	153 100+50+3
5.	252 200+50+2	18 10+8	65 60+5	392 300+90+2

NAME ______________

Lesson 2.1 Problem Solving

SHOW YOUR WORK

Solve each problem.

1. Circle the expanded form that expresses 213.

100 + 20 + 3

200 + 30 + 1

200 + 10 + 3

300 + 20 + 3

2. Shawn has 325 dollars. If Shawn uses only hundreds, tens, and ones, write the number of each kind of bill that Shawn has.

He has ___3___ hundred-dollar bills.

He has ___2___ ten-dollar bills.

He has ___5___ one-dollar bills.

3. Adriana has two hundred-dollar bills and three ten-dollar bills. How much money does Adriana have?

The two hundred-dollar bills are worth ___200___ dollars.

The three ten-dollar bills are worth ___30___ dollars.

Since there are ___0___ one-dollar bills, the ones place will have a ___0___.

Adriana has ___230___ dollars.

4. Bruce is playing with a set of base-ten blocks. He has 65 ten-blocks and 7 one-blocks. What is the value of his-blocks?

He can use ___65___ ten-blocks to represent ___6___ hundred blocks.

The value of his blocks is ___657___.

81,000+0+0+9

NAME ____________________

Lesson 2.2 Understanding Place Value (to ten thousands)

7 2 , 3 5 6

ten thousands, thousands, hundreds, tens, ones

The 2 has a value of 2 thousands or 2,000.

The 7 has a value of 7 ten thousands or 70,000.

Show the value of 5 in each number.

	a	b	c	d
1.	75,032 5,000	51,232 ______	365 ______	12,354 ______

Which digit is in the place named?

	a	b	c	d
2.	562 ones ____ is in the ones place.	35,961 hundreds ____ is in the hundreds place.	35,462 ten thousands ____ is in the ten thousands place.	46,123 thousands ____ is in the thousands place.

Name the place of the underlined digit.

	a	b	c	d
3.	<u>3</u>6,542 ____ is in the ________ place.	96,<u>4</u>91 ____ is in the ________ place.	1<u>2</u>,331 ____ is in the ________ place.	<u>6</u>51 ____ is in the ________ place.

Write each number in expanded form.

	a	b	c	d
4.	50,631 ________	12,560 ________	963 ________	43,561 ________
5.	81,009 ________	32,451 ________	6,320 ________	2,406 ________

6/23

NAME Elliott

Lesson 2.2 Problem Solving

SHOW YOUR WORK

Solve each problem.

1. Write the place value name for each digit in the number 542.

5 is in the __100__ place.

4 is in the __10__ place.

2 is in the __1__ place.

2. Write the number described. 8 is in the tens place. The digit in the ones place is three less than the digit in the tens place. The digit in the hundreds place is one-half the digit in the tens place. The digit in the thousands place is one more than the digit in the tens place. The digit in the ten thousands place is the same as the digit in the tens place.

__8__ is in the ten thousands place.

__9__ is in the thousands place.

__4__ is in the hundreds place.

__8__ is in the tens place.

__5__ is in the ones place.

The number is __89,485__.

3. Using the digits 5, 9, 1, 2, and 6, write the smallest number possible.

The smallest digit, __1__, will be in the __10__ place.

The greatest digit, __2__, will be in the __1__ place.

The smallest number possible using the digits 5, 9, 1, 2, and 6 is __12__.

4. Circle the number represented by 30,000 + 200 + 3.

30,233 32,300 30,203 32,003

1. 500 + 40 + 2 = 542

2. 89485

3.

4.

NAME ______________________

Lesson 2.3 Understanding Place Value (to hundred thousands)

4 6 2 , 3 5 1

- 4 — hundred thousands
- 6 — ten thousands
- 2 — thousands
- 3 — hundreds
- 5 — tens
- 1 — ones

Show the value of 2 in each number.

	a	b	c	d
1.	203,471	123,459	11,204	713,452
	200,000	______	______	______

Which digit is in the place named?

	a	b	c	d
2.	531,462 hundred thousands	62,496 hundreds	92,963 thousands	423,541 ten thousands
	___ is in the hundred thousands place.	___ is in the hundreds place.	___ is in the thousands place.	___ is in the ten thousands place.

Name the place of the underlined digit.

	a	b	c	d
3.	<u>4</u>51,679	9<u>6</u>,451	1<u>0</u>8,709	65<u>2</u>,982
	___ is in the ______ place.	___ is in the ______ place.	___ is in the ______ place.	___ is in the ______ place.

Write each number in expanded form.

	a	b	c	d
4.	600,981	730,104	80,360	91,123
	______	______	______	______
5.	123,456	98,731	103,407	605,431
	______	______	______	______

NAME ____________________

Lesson 2.3 Problem Solving

SHOW YOUR WORK

Solve each problem.

1. Write the number described:

0 is in the tens place, the thousands place, and the ten thousands place.

3 is in the ones place.

The digit in the hundreds place is three times the digit in the ones place.

The digit in the hundred thousands place is two times the digit in the ones place.

The number is __6__ __0__ __0__, __9__ __0__ __3__.

2. Alicia has 6 stacks of cards. Each stack of cards has a value. She has 2 cards in her stack of hundred thousands value cards. She has 5 ten thousands value cards. She has 2 thousands value cards. She has 9 hundreds value cards. Her stacks of tens value cards and ones value cards have 5 cards each. Write Alicia's card stacks in expanded form.

__2__ hundred thousands

__5__ ten thousands

__2__ thousands

__9__ hundreds

__5__ tens

__5__ ones

Expanded form:

200,000+ 50,000+2,000+900+50+5

3. Use the digits 3, 5, 7, 2, 9, and 1 to write the greatest number possible.

__97__

4. Use the digits 3, 5, 7, 2, 9, and 1 to write the smallest number possible.

__23__

NAME ______________________

Lesson 2.4 Greater Than, Less Than, or Equal To

Compare the numbers. Write <, >, or =.

< means "is less than."
> means "is greater than."
= means "is equal to."

If two numbers are not equal when comparing them, they are **unequal**. These comparisons are called **inequalities**.

Compare 36 and 92. Compare the value. Look at the biggest place value. In this case it would be the tens place. 3 tens is less than 9 tens.

36 "is less than" 92.

36 <u><</u> 92

Compare 193 and 122. Compare the value. Look at the hundreds place. Since the hundreds place is the same in both, look at the tens place. 9 tens "is greater than" 2 tens.

193 <u>></u> 122

Compare each pair of numbers. Write <, >, or =.

	a	b	c	d
1.	3,342 ___ 3,339	305 ___ 272	200 ___ 200	180 ___ 810
2.	352 ___ 357	75 ___ 70	186 ___ 286	910 ___ 910
3.	1,964 ___ 1,694	3,721 ___ 986	2,545 ___ 2,541	183 ___ 189

Circle the greatest number.

	a	b	c	d
4.	9,000 900 9	32 23 67	10 1,100 110	3 7 11
5.	25 27 17	86 54 16	80,001 80,100 810	323 232 131

SHOW YOUR WORK

Solve each problem.

6. Andy has 4 ten-dollar bills and 5 one-dollar bills. Sheila has 3 ten-dollar bills and 15 one-dollar bills. Henry has 8 ten-dollar bills and 4 one-dollar bills. Who has the same amount of money?

   ___Andy___ and ___Sheila___ have the same amount of money.

7. Enrique has 7 comic books. Adelina has 2 more comic books than Enrique. Susana has 4 fewer comic books than Enrique. Who has the most comic books?

   ___Adelina___ has the most comic books.

6.

7.

NAME ____________________

Lesson 2.5 Rounding

The steps for rounding are:

1) Look one place to the right of the digit you wish to round.
2) If the digit is less than 5, leave the digit in the rounding place as it is, and change the digits to the right of the rounding place to zero.
3) If the digit is 5 or greater, add 1 to the digit in the rounding place, and change the digits to the right of the rounding place to zero.

Round 5,432 to the nearest thousand. 5 is in the thousands place. Look at the 4. Do not change the 5. 5,432 to the nearest thousand is 5,000.

Round each number to the nearest ten.

	a	b	c	d
1.	963 ______	154 ______	186 ______	4,031 ______
2.	125 ______	3,452 ______	8,657 ______	7,987 ______

Round each number to the nearest hundred.

	a	b	c	d
3.	8,765 ______	986 ______	3,250 ______	7,913 ______
4.	507 ______	1,349 ______	842 ______	4,370 ______

Round each number to the place named.

	a	b	c	d
5.	8,576 hundreds ______	1,930 thousands ______	364 tens ______	1,543 tens ______
6.	1,886 hundreds ______	765 tens ______	863 hundreds ______	86 tens ______
7.	451 tens ______	8,713 tens ______	472 hundreds ______	5,325 tens ______
8.	3,651 thousands ______	123 tens ______	486 tens ______	2,356 hundreds ______

NAME ____________________

Check What You Learned

Numeration through 100,000

Show the value of 2 in each number.

	a	b	c	d
1.	32	250	10,251	92,054
	____	____	____	____
2.	629	4,527	27,531	43,592
	____	____	____	____

What digit is in the place named?

	a	b	c	d
3.	321 hundreds	5,412 tens	9,865 thousands	796 ones
	____	____	____	____

Name the place of the underlined digit.

	a	b	c	d
4.	75,361	8,904	865	987
	____ is in the ____ place.	____ is in the ____ place.	____ is in the ____ place.	____ is in the ____ place.

Write each number in expanded form.

	a	b	c	d
5.	592	4,532	4,907	16,983
	____	____	____	____
6.	10,700	180,982	90,531	63
	____	____	____	____

CHAPTER 2 POSTTEST

Check What You Learned

Numeration through 100,000

Compare each pair of numbers. Write <, >, or =.

	a	b	c	d
7.	52 ___ 96	5 ___ 8	73 ___ 72	980 ___ 970

Circle the greatest number.

	a	b	c	d
8.	16 15 17	29 32 29	76 760 67	13 93 102

Circle the smallest number.

	a	b	c	d
9.	23 96 21	56 92 82	20 30 40	16 16 14

Round each number to the place named.

	a	b	c	d
10.	592 hundreds ______	86 tens ______	5,432 thousands ______	981 tens ______

SHOW YOUR WORK

Solve each problem.

11. What is the greatest number that you can write using the digits 0, 7, 4, 6, and 3?

The greatest number is ________.

12. Circle the number represented by 4,000 + 30 in expanded form.

400,030 404,330 4,030 4,303

13. Luke wants to buy a radio that costs 37 dollars plus sales tax. Round the cost of the radio to the tens place to see how much money Luke should bring to the store to cover the cost of the radio and the sales tax.

Luke should bring ________ dollars to the store.

11.

12.

13.

CHAPTER 2 POSTTEST

NAME ____________________

Check What You Know

Adding and Subtracting 2- and 3-Digit Numbers (with renaming)

Add.

	a	b	c	d	e	f
1.	27 + 43	86 + 92	[illegible]	[illegible]	45 + 154	87 + 196
2.	387 + 405	786 + 193	150 + 270	863 + 42	323 + 46	76 + 84
3.	132 + 196	46 + 231	87 + 121	76 + 93	23 + 54	186 + 231
4.	65 + 15	28 + 93	57 + 761	192 + 775	423 + 176	23 + 45

Subtract.

	a	b	c	d	e	f
5.	123 − 15	87 − 23	545 − 35	79 − 63	187 − 93	782 − 143
6.	898 − 454	763 − 321	981 − 133	725 − 123	805 − 73	120 − 80
7.	76 − 41	87 − 35	72 − 35	153 − 92	763 − 154	876 − 450
8.	879 − 69	87 − 43	100 − 35	730 − 300	765 − 231	845 − 708

NAME ____________________

Check What You Know

SHOW YOUR WORK

Adding and Subtracting 2- and 3-Digit Numbers (with renaming)

CHAPTER 3 PRETEST

Solve each problem.

9. Kurt has saved 29 dollars to buy a remote control car. The remote control car that he wants to buy costs 43 dollars. How much more money does he need to save?

Are you to add or subtract? __add__

He will need to save __14__ more dollars.

10. Latisha sold 36 candy bars on Friday and 45 candy bars on Saturday. How many candy bars did she sell in all?

Are you to add or subtract? __add__

Latisha sold __81__ candy bars in all.

11. Harry had 57 pennies and 16 dimes. How many coins does he have?

Are you to add or subtract? __add__

He has __73__ coins.

12. Tawna has 253 pennies. Shawn has 146 pennies. How many more pennies does Tawna have than Shawn?

Tawna has __117__ more pennies than Shawn.

13. The team sold 453 tickets for the game. There were 249 adult tickets sold. How many children's tickets were sold?

The team sold __214__ children's tickets.

9.

10.

11.

12.

13.

NAME ______________________________

Lesson 3.1 Adding 2-Digit Numbers

	Add the ones.	Add the tens.	
75 + 66	1 (carried) 75 + 66 = …1	1 (carried) 75 addend + 66 addend	141 sum

$5 + 6 = 11$

Add.

	a	b	c	d	e	f
1.	23 + 95 = 118	17 + 86	90 + 50	72 + 46	87 + 23	97 + 65
2.	19 + 75	26 + 93	47 + 58	54 + 59	64 + 94	87 + 27
3.	23 + 79	38 + 81	75 + 86	23 + 92	86 + 41	39 + 82
4.	43 + 71	65 + 39	37 + 82	19 + 83	43 + 62	75 + 95
5.	60 + 40	20 + 87	23 + 97	26 + 85	94 + 45	23 + 63
6.	67 + 72	95 + 92	83 + 67	49 + 69	27 + 99	82 + 57

NAME ____________________

Lesson 3.1 Problem Solving

SHOW YOUR WORK

Solve each problem.

1. Sarah earned 58 dollars last week from her paper route. This week she earned 47 dollars. How much money did she earn for both weeks combined?

She earned ___58___ dollars last week.

She earned ___47___ dollars this week.

She earned ___95___ dollars for both weeks combined.

1.

2. Eduardo has 72 dollars in his savings account. How much money will be in his savings account if he deposits 43 dollars today?

He has ___72___ dollars.

He will deposit ___43___ dollars.

He will have a total of ___29___ dollars in his savings account.

2.

3. Flo read a book with 92 pages. Sofia read a book with 87 pages. How many pages did they both read?

Flo read ___92___ pages.

Sofia read ___87___ pages.

Together they read ___179___ pages.

3.

4. At the wedding reception there were 77 adults and 52 children. How many people were at the wedding reception?

There were ___77___ adults.

There were ___52___ children.

There were ___129___ people at the wedding reception.

4.

NAME ____________

Lesson 3.2 Subtracting 2 Digits from 3 Digits

	Subtract the ones.	To subtract the tens, rename the 1 hundred and 2 tens as "12 tens."	Subtract the tens.	
125 − 84	125 − 84 1	~~1~~ ~~2~~ (12) 5 − 84 1	~~1~~ ~~2~~ (12) 5 − 84 41	minuend subtrahend difference

Subtract.

	a	b	c	d	e	f
1.	173 − 33	121 − 60	195 − 44	122 − 11	147 − 53	182 − 90
2.	143 − 62	180 − 70	119 − 15	123 − 12	186 − 65	187 − 42
3.	154 − 13	127 − 83	187 − 67	135 − 42	115 − 24	171 − 60
4.	132 − 51	177 − 43	192 − 71	186 − 92	134 − 72	125 − 45
5.	129 − 86	176 − 75	120 − 40	194 − 53	189 − 62	134 − 42
6.	165 − 51	167 − 45	150 − 30	157 − 63	149 − 61	139 − 62
7.	175 − 82	167 − 43	133 − 41	148 − 78	165 − 43	128 − 57

NAME ____________________

Lesson 3.2 Subtracting 2 Digits from 3 Digits

	Rename 5 tens and 3 ones as "4 tens and 13 ones."	Subtract the ones.	Rename 1 hundred and 4 tens as "14 tens."	Subtract the tens.	
153	1 $\overset{4}{\cancel{5}}$ $\overset{13}{\cancel{3}}$	1 $\overset{4}{\cancel{5}}$ $\overset{13}{\cancel{3}}$	$\overset{14}{\cancel{1}\cancel{5}}$ $\overset{13}{\cancel{3}}$	$\overset{14}{\cancel{1}\cancel{5}}$ $\overset{13}{\cancel{3}}$	minuend
− 65	− 65	− 65	− 65	− 65	subtrahend
		8	8	88	difference

Subtract.

	a	b	c	d	e	f
1.	162 − 73	175 − 97	182 − 94	103 − 17	116 − 39	127 − 88
2.	174 − 95	147 − 68	132 − 65	115 − 49	107 − 39	181 − 95
3.	101 − 75	100 − 92	127 − 79	133 − 44	142 − 73	135 − 47
4.	141 − 63	137 − 79	142 − 73	153 − 67	155 − 96	164 − 88
5.	100 − 72	106 − 48	117 − 88	124 − 66	163 − 89	180 − 93
6.	172 − 87	181 − 92	145 − 66	132 − 57	130 − 43	120 − 62
7.	164 − 85	152 − 63	144 − 87	157 − 69	123 − 45	174 − 87

NAME ______________

Lesson 3.2 Subtracting 2 Digits from 3 Digits

Subtract.

	a	b	c	d	e	f
1.	132 − 71	196 − 87	165 − 59	163 − 71	119 − 29	107 − 76
2.	106 − 51	100 − 29	153 − 69	147 − 88	192 − 75	173 − 62
3.	175 − 95	169 − 99	142 − 37	140 − 93	131 − 57	123 − 45
4.	167 − 76	173 − 82	192 − 95	143 − 77	126 − 54	119 − 38
5.	117 − 26	100 − 33	175 − 46	142 − 57	136 − 47	121 − 32
6.	176 − 89	143 − 54	140 − 39	173 − 75	163 − 92	159 − 46
7.	144 − 86	122 − 31	191 − 75	175 − 93	144 − 65	136 − 42
8.	121 − 37	106 − 42	165 − 43	162 − 47	181 − 57	169 − 82
9.	106 − 99	127 − 49	136 − 58	124 − 75	143 − 52	182 − 95

NAME ______________________

Lesson 3.2 Problem Solving

SHOW YOUR WORK

Solve each problem.

1. There are 119 houses on Green Street. The postal carrier has only 57 flyers to deliver to Green Street. How many more flyers does he need?

The postal carrier needs __________ flyers.

He has __________ flyers.

He needs __________ more flyers.

2. There are 162 days of school in a school year. This year, David has gone to school for 54 days. How many more days will David need to go to school?

There are __________ days of school.

David has gone to __________ days of school.

David needs to go to school for __________ more days.

3. Ivanna has 117 pennies. She buys a candy bar for 59 pennies. How many pennies does she have left?

Ivanna has __________ pennies.

She spent __________ pennies.

She has __________ pennies left.

4. There are 153 students in third grade. If 62 students did not go on the field trip to the zoo, how many students did go on the field trip?

There are __________ students in the third grade.

__________ students did not go on the field trip.

__________ students went on the field trip.

NAME ____________________

Lesson 3.3 Adding 3-Digit Numbers

	Add the ones.	Add the tens.	Add the hundreds.
$\begin{array}{r} 755 \\ +469 \\ \hline \end{array}$	$\begin{array}{r} \overset{1}{7}\,5\,5 \\ +469 \\ \hline 4 \end{array}$	$\begin{array}{r} 755 \\ +469 \\ \hline 24 \end{array}$	$\begin{array}{r} 755 \\ +\ 469 \\ \hline 1224 \end{array}$

Add.

	a	b	c	d	e	f
1.	123 + 562 = 685	982 + 171	342 + 591	782 + 341	123 + 321	681 + 975
2.	862 + 313	900 + 130	720 + 850	931 + 111	823 + 457	547 + 321
3.	861 + 421	862 + 139	431 + 250	782 + 191	751 + 605	871 + 323
4.	791 + 191	144 + 800	192 + 175	257 + 147	203 + 211	541 + 693
5.	705 + 719	641 + 209	873 + 505	700 + 650	105 + 341	450 + 362
6.	593 + 741	861 + 209	735 + 145	820 + 431	738 + 387	719 + 120
7.	153 + 312	712 + 210	619 + 715	205 + 316	153 + 814	613 + 261

NAME ______________________

Lesson 3.3 Problem Solving

SHOW YOUR WORK

Solve each problem.

1. At the basketball game, 232 adult tickets were sold and 179 children's tickets were sold. How many tickets were sold for the basketball game?

There were 232 adult tickets sold.

There were 179 children's tickets sold.

There were 411 total tickets sold.

2. At the local elementary school there are 543 boys and 476 girls. How many total students are there?

There are 543 boys.

There are 476 girls.

There are 1019 total students.

3. Mr. Gomez has 639 blue tiles and 722 green tiles. How many blue and green tiles does Mr. Gomez have?

Mr. Gomez has 639 blue tiles.

He has 722 green tiles.

He has 361 blue and green tiles.

4. The shoe store has 324 pairs of athletic shoes and 187 pairs of sandals. How many athletic shoes and sandals does the shoe store have in all?

There are 328 pairs of athletic shoes.

There are 187 pairs of sandals.

There are 406 pairs of athletic shoes and sandals in all.

1.
2.
3.
4.

NAME ____________________

Lesson 3.4 Subtracting 3-Digit Numbers

Rename 2 tens and 1 one as "1 ten and 11 ones." Then, subtract the ones.	Rename 6 hundreds and 1 ten as "5 hundreds and 11 tens." Then, subtract the tens.	Subtract the hundreds.

$$\begin{array}{r} 621 \\ -259 \\ \hline \end{array} \qquad \begin{array}{r} {\scriptstyle 1\,11} \\ 62\not{1} \\ -259 \\ \hline 2 \end{array} \qquad \begin{array}{r} {\scriptstyle 11} \\ {\scriptstyle 5\,\not{1}\,11} \\ \not{6}\not{2}\not{1} \\ -259 \\ \hline 62 \end{array} \qquad \begin{array}{r} {\scriptstyle 11} \\ {\scriptstyle 5\,\not{1}\,11} \\ \not{6}\not{2}\not{1} \\ -259 \\ \hline 362 \end{array} \begin{array}{l} \text{minuend} \\ \text{subtrahend} \\ \text{difference} \end{array}$$

Subtract.

	a	b	c	d	e	f
1.	321 − 109 = 212	745 − 152	639 − 150	830 − 710	626 − 146	457 − 309
2.	729 − 321	657 − 451	386 − 107	411 − 305	486 − 109	311 − 121
3.	983 − 652	971 − 572	876 − 357	549 − 360	721 − 144	958 − 637
4.	256 − 142	347 − 139	725 − 196	863 − 692	980 − 532	720 − 500
5.	543 − 457	762 − 135	132 − 107	921 − 571	631 − 545	982 − 144
6.	531 − 250	720 − 371	582 − 357	793 − 457	612 − 483	592 − 107

NAME ______________________

Lesson 3.4 Problem Solving

SHOW YOUR WORK

Solve each problem.

1. There are 990 seats at the stadium. If there are 587 people at the stadium, how many empty seats are there?

There are __990__ stadium seats.

There are __587__ people.

There are __403__ empty seats.

2. A bicycle cost 530 dollars. There is a rebate for 147 dollars. How much will the bike cost after the rebate?

The bicycle costs __530__ dollars.

The rebate is __147__ dollars.

The cost of the bicycle after the rebate is __383__ dollars.

3. There were 600 green and yellow paper clips in the package. If 230 were green, how many were yellow?

There were a total of __600__ paper clips.

There were __230__ green paper clips.

There were __370__ yellow paper clips.

4. The ice cream store sold 349 scoops of ice cream on Monday. The store sold 178 scoops of ice cream on Tuesday. How many more scoops did the store sell on Monday?

The ice cream store sold __229__ more scoops on Monday than on Tuesday.

5. Last year, Randy received a set of 360 toy cars. This year, Randy counted only 163 toy cars in his set. How many toy cars had Randy lost?

Randy lost __197__ toy cars.

1. 990 − 587 = 403

2. 530 − 147 = 383

3. 600 − 230 = 370

4. 349 − 178 = 229

5. 360 − 163 = 197

NAME ____________________

Lesson 3.5 Thinking Subtraction for Addition

To check
215 + 109 = 324,
subtract 109 from 324.

$$\begin{array}{r} 215 \\ +109 \\ \hline 324 \\ -109 \\ \hline 215 \end{array}$$

These should be the same.

Add. Check each answer.

	a	b	c	d	e	f
1.	157 + 212 = 369; 369 − 212 = 157	719 + 182	312 + 105	213 + 519	306 + 215	120 + 170
2.	710 + 398	357 + 249	712 + 363	714 + 291	312 + 85	419 + 57
3.	300 + 547	591 + 120	612 + 319	425 + 125	411 + 120	247 + 259
4.	863 + 192	459 + 130	603 + 209	711 + 191	252 + 130	412 + 283

NAME ______________________

Lesson 3.6 Thinking Addition for Subtraction

To check
982 − 657 = 325,
add 657 to 325.

```
  982  <---┐
 -657      |
 ----      |
  325      These should be the same.
 +657      |
 ----      |
  982  <---┘
```

Subtract. Check each answer.

	a	b	c	d	e	f
1.	720 − 150 = 570; check: 570 + 150 = 720	321 − 83	125 − 92	983 − 657	456 − 291	442 − 220
2.	300 − 179	119 − 104	423 − 197	259 − 147	592 − 463	708 − 412
3.	519 − 120	540 − 320	192 − 86	710 − 447	683 − 419	712 − 307
4.	719 − 532	919 − 457	687 − 250	912 − 609	542 − 327	728 − 530

NAME ____________________

Lesson 3.7 Addition and Subtraction Practice

Add or subtract.

	a	b	c	d	e	f
1.	39 + 92	86 + 93	132 − 41	186 − 92	543 − 121	125 + 89
2.	76 + 192	154 − 92	543 − 206	150 − 90	650 + 129	920 − 860
3.	137 + 310	159 − 82	185 − 96	432 − 257	710 − 512	819 − 720
4.	541 + 862	432 − 119	720 + 140	186 − 107	540 − 75	413 + 356
5.	812 + 93	712 − 347	690 − 320	451 − 253	512 − 308	803 + 112
6.	119 + 104	703 + 219	861 − 172	186 + 210	513 − 211	179 − 86
7.	120 − 45	198 − 79	312 − 192	519 + 130	710 + 195	712 − 419
8.	412 − 306	790 − 205	157 + 192	175 − 84	192 + 210	786 − 442
9.	510 + 834	674 − 556	700 − 310	120 + 460	690 − 541	710 − 82

NAME ____________________

Lesson 3.8 Addition and Subtraction Practice

Add or subtract.

	a	b	c	d	e	f
1.	72 +59	76 +82	138 − 52	192 − 75	310 +354	763 −123
2.	191 +210	583 −421	710 −190	54 +86	93 +104	210 −108
3.	582 +529	711 −547	712 − 92	860 +139	786 −457	259 +457
4.	186 +211	210 −102	96 +87	310 + 99	386 +503	710 −605
5.	232 −144	457 −310	386 +205	740 −310	862 −456	415 −209
6.	392 − 86	510 − 47	610 −232	192 − 86	191 +212	138 +493
7.	205 +472	437 +291	186 +396	408 +520	393 −121	683 −541
8.	386 −130	149 +310	186 − 93	110 +342	186 − 90	310 +620
9.	130 +210	190 − 70	163 +292	145 + 96	192 + 47	186 + 57

NAME ____________________

Check What You Learned

Adding and Subtracting 2- and 3-Digit Numbers (with renaming)

Add.

	a	b	c	d	e	f
1.	75 + 92	135 + 210	193 + 56	310 + 92	513 + 409	746 + 122
2.	193 + 86	183 + 192	842 + 908	109 + 236	963 + 310	150 + 210
3.	512 + 457	310 + 97	510 + 346	910 + 132	512 + 403	912 + 78
4.	543 + 286	123 + 592	647 + 382	442 + 85	123 + 210 + 392	212 + 391 + 407

Subtract.

	a	b	c	d	e	f
5.	172 − 35	192 − 86	174 − 96	120 − 80	310 − 40	293 − 107
6.	986 − 698	862 − 245	352 − 121	187 − 72	647 − 253	547 − 183
7.	662 − 503	708 − 231	456 − 269	882 − 199	753 − 268	712 − 543
8.	712 − 402	548 − 213	593 − 369	610 − 132	782 − 441	192 − 85

CHAPTER 3 POSTTEST

NAME ______________________

Check What You Learned

SHOW YOUR WORK

Adding and Subtracting 2- and 3-Digit Numbers (with renaming)

Solve each problem.

9. For a game of checkers, 24 checkers are needed. There are only 18 checkers in the box. How many checkers are missing?

There are ____6____ checkers missing.

10. An adult has 32 teeth. A child has 24 teeth. How many more teeth does the adult have?

An adult has __________ more teeth than a child.

11. Sam weighed 232 pounds. He lost 13 pounds. How much does Sam weigh now?

Sam weighs __________ pounds.

12. Alvin has 532 pennies. Regina has 691 pennies. How many pennies do they have together?

Alvin and Regina have __________ pennies together.

13. Mr. Ito is 53 years old. His daughter, Kimi, is 25. How much older is Mr. Ito than his daughter?

Mr. Ito is __________ years older than his daughter.

14. Mr. and Mrs. Acosta have been married for 47 years. Mrs. Acosta was 29 when she married Mr. Acosta. How old is Mrs. Acosta now?

Mrs. Acosta is __________ years old.

9.

10.

11.

12.

13.

14.

CHAPTER 3 POSTTEST

NAME ____________________

Check What You Know

Adding and Subtracting to 4 Digits (with renaming)

Add or subtract.

	a	b	c	d	e
1.	13 7 +19	23 42 +97	22 24 +16	8 9 +5	21 47 +58
2.	123 415 +423	190 180 +360	420 567 +321	519 612 +313	423 521 +747
3.	1436 +5120	5190 +4125	5032 +1764	4321 +2841	5960 +4011
4.	3121 +1076	1300 +2900	4320 +1051	1905 +1706	5190 +3049
5.	1340 − 380	1960 − 420	720 −340	5120 −1780	4963 −1082
6.	5947 −4272	5803 −1992	1906 −1173	1876 − 759	4120 −3290
7.	9645 −6823	312 − 20	421 − 30	1500 −1200	4500 − 720
8.	860 −729	9120 −7210	8160 −2400	4242 − 963	4163 −3552

NAME ____________________

CHAPTER 4 PRETEST

Check What You Know

Adding and Subtracting to 4 Digits (with renaming)

SHOW YOUR WORK

Solve each problem.

9. Gerod has 5 birds, 3 turtles, 2 hamsters, and 1 dog. How many pets does he have?

Gerod has __11__ pets.

10. Oleta has 19 dimes, 27 quarters, 153 pennies, and 6 nickels. How many coins does she have?

Oleta has __205__ coins.

11. James received 100 dollars for his birthday. He spent 63 dollars of it on two computer games. How much money does he have left?

James has __77__ dollars left.

12. At a basketball game, one team scored 36 points. The other team scored 27 points. How many total points were scored in the game?

There were a total of __63__ points scored in the basketball game.

13. In the year 1998, an antique vase was 239 years old. In what year was the vase made?

The vase was made in the year __1759__.

14. During his walk each day, Paul counted his steps. In 4 days, he walked 420, 980, 642, and 760 steps. How many steps did he walk?

Paul walked __2,802__ steps in 4 days.

420 + 980 = 1,400; 1,400 + 642 = 2,042; 2,042 + 760 = 2,802

NAME ______________________

Lesson 4.1 Adding 3 or More Numbers (1- and 2-digit)

Add the ones. Add the tens.

45	5		¹45	¹45
62	2	7	62	62
+94	+4	+ 4	+94	+ 94
		11 or 10 + 1	1	201

Add.

	a	b	c	d	e	f
1.	3 6 +9 18	7 5 +8	6 12 +13	8 17 +19	12 32 +53	8 6 +2
2.	17 93 +23	16 45 +92	82 18 +23	7 19 +57	22 86 +34	50 40 +60
3.	86 93 +72	23 35 +62	18 35 +67	86 54 +83	32 49 +76	13 19 +23
4.	25 66 +72	81 19 +83	53 42 +93	13 12 +14	10 20 +90	82 76 +54
5.	86 54 32 +52	92 10 53 +47	81 71 36 +27	12 18 24 +19	93 48 13 +27	41 86 53 +22

NAME ____________________

Lesson 4.1 Problem Solving

SHOW YOUR WORK

Solve each problem.

1. The bubble gum dispenser has 23 blue gumballs, 16 red gumballs, 14 yellow gumballs, and 7 green gumballs. How many gumballs are in the dispenser?

There are __________ blue gumballs.

There are __________ red gumballs.

There are __________ yellow gumballs.

There are __________ green gumballs.

There are __________ gumballs in the dispenser.

2. In the fruit basket there are 9 apples, 6 bananas, and 7 oranges. How many pieces of fruit are in the fruit basket?

There are __________ apples.

There are __________ bananas.

There are __________ oranges.

There are __________ pieces of fruit in the basket.

3. Mr. Williams is 53 years old. Mrs. Williams is 44 years old. Their son is 18 years old. What is the combined total of the ages of the Williams family?

Mr. Williams is __________ years old.

Mrs. Williams is __________ years old.

Their son is __________ years old.

The total of their ages is __________ years.

4. When Hailey went shopping for school supplies, she bought a calculator for 14 dollars, a package of paper for 5 dollars, a calendar for 3 dollars, and a package of pens for 3 dollars. How much did Hailey spend on school supplies?

Hailey spent __________ dollars on school supplies.

1.

2.

3.

4.

NAME ____________________

Lesson 4.2 Adding 3 or More Numbers (3-digit)

	Add the ones.	Add the tens.	Add the hundreds.
231 457 +625	231 457 +625 3	231 457 +625 13	231 457 +625 1313

Add.

	a	b	c	d	e	f
1.	522 367 +151 1040	868 321 +405 4	150 200 +300	701 231 +862	986 105 +525	129 318 +467
2.	803 623 +186	545 309 +119	868 740 +809	132 195 +118	200 300 +600	180 240 +303
3.	861 757 +409	863 404 +891	731 356 +402	865 591 +217	238 405 +596	898 777 +192
4.	341 127 +192	864 425 +323	127 291 +867	205 876 +198	712 490 +600	750 400 +203
5.	591 603 907 +432	862 191 183 +251	892 645 320 +123	132 169 119 +105	323 309 452 +690	712 613 518 +437

NAME ______________________

Lesson 4.2 Problem Solving

SHOW YOUR WORK

Solve each problem.

1. Joe earned 135 dollars during his first week of work. He earned 213 dollars during his second week of work. He earned 159 dollars during his third week of work. How much money did Joe earn during the three weeks that he worked?

Joe earned _____ dollars during his first week.

Joe earned _____ dollars during his second week.

Joe earned _____ dollars during his third week.

Joe earned _____ dollars for all 3 weeks of work.

2. On the first floor of a 3-story apartment building, there are 186 apartments occupied. On the second floor, there are 175 apartments occupied. On the third floor, there are 182 apartments occupied. How many apartments are occupied in all?

There are _____ apartments occupied on the first floor.

There are _____ apartments occupied on the second floor.

There are _____ apartments occupied on the third floor.

There are _____ apartments occupied in all.

3. The following numbers of students attend four different schools: 543, 692, 487, and 603. How many students attend all four schools?

________ students attend all four schools.

4. In a book, chapter 1 has 112 pages and chapter 2 has 119 pages. Chapter 3 has 103 pages and chapter 4 has 108 pages. How many pages are in the book?

There are _____ pages in the book.

1.

2.

3.

4.

NAME ____________________

Lesson 4.3 Adding 4-Digit Numbers

	Add the ones.	Add the tens.	Add the hundreds.	Add the thousands.
3746 + 5899	3746 + 5899 = 5	3746 + 5899 = 45	3746 + 5899 = 645	3746 + 5899 = 9645

Add.

	a	b	c	d	e	f
1.	7865 + 1192 = 9057	8654 + 1219	4320 + 3069	3543 + 3921	4293 + 5176	6405 + 3398
2.	1982 + 1782	7083 + 2907	4325 + 4986	6057 + 1239	8761 + 1032	2305 + 5747
3.	3050 + 4707	6932 + 2349	5437 + 2968	1718 + 2347	7923 + 1250	4523 + 3962
4.	5431 + 2989	7986 + 1479	1119 + 2459	7239 + 1635	2450 + 7267	6527 + 2985
5.	5431 + 1982	7986 + 1246	1543 + 3989	7121 + 1923	8763 + 1005	4321 + 2387
6.	5450 + 1987	4733 + 2576	3981 + 2877	6986 + 2928	7181 + 2111	7900 + 2005

NAME ______________________

Lesson 4.3 Problem Solving

SHOW YOUR WORK

Solve each problem.

1. Two local high schools have 1,523 students and 1,695 students. How many students are there at both high schools together?

One high school has __________ students.

The other high school has __________students.

There are a total of __________ students at both high schools.

2. Monica started at an elevation of 1,200 feet for her hiking trip. She hiked up the mountain for 1,320 feet in elevation. How high did she hike?

Monica started at __________ feet in elevation.

She hiked __________ feet in elevation.

She hiked up to an elevation of __________ feet.

3. Steve has a coin worth 1,050 dollars. He has another coin worth 1,072 dollars. How much are both coins worth?

Both coins are worth __________ dollars.

4. Roy ran 1,100 yards as a running back during his junior year of high school. During his senior year of high school, he ran 1,500 yards as a running back. How many yards did he run in both years combined?

Roy ran a total of __________ yards for both his junior and senior year of high school.

1.

2.

3.

4.

NAME ____________________

Lesson 4.4 Subtracting to 4 Digits

	Subtract the ones.	Rename 4 hundreds and 3 tens as "3 hundreds and 13 tens." Subtract the tens.	Rename 5 thousands and 3 hundreds as "4 thousands and 13 hundreds." Subtract the hundreds.	Subtract the thousands.
5437 −1592	5437 −1592 5	3 13 5~~4~~~~3~~7 −1592 45	13 4 ~~3~~ 13 ~~5~~~~4~~~~3~~7 −1592 845	13 4 ~~3~~ 13 ~~5~~~~4~~~~3~~7 −1592 3845

Subtract.

	a	b	c	d	e
1.	9865 −2382 7483	7528 − 792	8654 −3993	1925 − 183	1876 − 982
2.	5473 −3591	8762 − 682	7945 − 963	8654 − 772	7846 −3974
3.	6932 −2840	1389 − 794	2545 − 963	7863 −2572	8121 − 640
4.	7865 − 974	3456 − 661	7982 − 490	8163 −4670	4325 −1534
5.	9876 − 985	8716 −5823	5432 −3651	3287 − 395	7805 − 164
6.	5439 − 767	4321 − 841	7865 − 974	7976 −4682	5439 − 866

NAME ____________________

Lesson 4.4 Problem Solving

SHOW YOUR WORK

Solve each problem.

1. There are 2,532 students at the school. 1,341 are girls. How many are boys?

There are ________ students.

There are ________ girls.

There are ________ boys.

2. In 2003, the average rent for a house was 1,250 dollars per month. In 1944, the average rent for a house was 495 dollars per month. How much higher was the rent in 2003 than in 1944?

Rent in 2003 was ________ dollars per month.

Rent in 1944 was ________ dollars per month.

Rent in 2003 was ________ dollars per month higher than in 1944.

3. In the year 1986, Mrs. Olveras turned 103 years old. In what year was she born?

In the year ________,

Mrs. Olveras turned ________ years old.

Mrs. Olveras was born in ________.

4. In the year 1996, Mr. Smith's car was considered a classic. The car was made in 1942. How old is Mr. Smith's car?

Mr. Smith's car is ________ years old.

5. Kayla wants to visit her grandmother who lives 2,583 miles away. The airplane will only take her 2,392 miles toward her destination. Kayla needs to rent a car to drive the remaining miles. How many miles does Kayla need to drive?

Kayla would need to drive ________ miles.

1.

2.

3.

4.

5.

NAME ____________________

Lesson 4.5 Estimating Addition

Round each number to the highest place value the numbers have in common. Then, add from right to left.

$$\begin{array}{r} 194 \\ +\ 76 \\ \hline \end{array} \rightarrow \begin{array}{r} 190 \\ +\ 80 \\ \hline 270 \end{array}$$

The highest place value for 194 and 76 is the tens place. Round 194 and 76 to the tens place. Add.

$$\begin{array}{r} 203 \\ +196 \\ \hline \end{array} \rightarrow \begin{array}{r} 200 \\ +200 \\ \hline 400 \end{array}$$

The highest place value for 203 and 196 is the hundreds place. Round 203 and 196 to the hundreds place. Add.

Estimate each sum.

	a		b	c	d
1.	25 + 36	30 + 40 = 70	23 + 14	57 + 51	42 + 92
2.	92 + 51		131 + 42	165 + 92	147 + 97
3.	147 + 362	100 + 400 = 500	175 + 302	457 + 603	543 + 261
4.	1132 + 432		1250 + 347	5786 + 432	4679 + 578
5.	1562 + 3492	2000 + 3000 = 5000	6054 + 6542	3541 + 7987	2795 + 2454

NAME ____________________

Lesson 4.5 Problem Solving

SHOW YOUR WORK

Solve each problem by using estimation.

1. Kirima read 534 pages last week and 352 pages this week. About how many pages did Kirima read?

Kirima read about __________ pages.

2. Tim has 13 dollars. James has 15 dollars. About how many dollars do they have together?

Tim and James have about __________ dollars together.

3. Mr. Hwan had 532 dollars in his savings account before he made a deposit of 259 dollars. About how much money does he have in his savings account now?

Mr. Hwan has about __________ dollars in his savings account now.

4. Mrs. Luna is 43 years old. Mrs. Turner is 52 years old. Mrs. Rockwell is 39 years old. About how much is their combined age?

Their combined age is about __________ years.

5. Marla bought 4 boards at the home center. The boards were 86, 103, 152, and 161 inches long. About how many inches of boards did Marla buy?

Marla bought about __________ inches of boards.

1.

2.

3.

4.

5.

NAME ____________________

Lesson 4.6 Estimating Subtraction

Round each number to the highest place value the numbers have in common. Then, subtract from right to left.

236 → 240		396 → 400	
− 49 → − 50		−287 → −300	
190		100	

The highest place value for 236 and 49 is the tens place. Round 236 and 49 to the tens place. Subtract.

The highest place value for 396 and 287 is the hundreds place. Round 396 and 287 to the hundreds place. Subtract.

Estimate each difference.

	a		b	c	d
1.	56 − 43	60 − 40 = 20	49 − 12	72 − 61	80 − 45
2.	451 − 72		986 − 59	760 − 32	542 − 57
3.	543 − 290	500 − 300 = 200	943 − 457	547 − 249	686 − 162
4.	1543 − 661		3247 − 843	4560 − 493	7631 − 647
5.	8798 − 4453	9000 − 4000 = 5000	9476 − 2652	7345 − 6443	9432 − 1486

NAME ___________________

Lesson 4.6 Problem Solving

SHOW YOUR WORK

Solve each problem by using estimation.

1. Fred had 39 dollars. He gave 23 dollars to Kim. About how much money does Fred have left?

Fred has about _________ dollars left.

2. There are 186 apartments in an apartment building. 92 are not rented. About how many apartments are rented?

There are about _________ rented apartments.

3. Sue wants to buy a bicycle for 560 dollars. She has 430 dollars. About how much more money does she need to buy the bicycle?

Sue needs about _________ more dollars to buy the bicycle.

4. At the theater, 98 adult tickets were sold. If 210 tickets were sold, about how many children's tickets were sold?

About _________ children's tickets were sold.

5. Kelly bought a roll of cloth 197 inches long. She cut 85 inches off the roll to use in a project. About how many inches did she have left on the roll?

Kelly had about _________ inches left on the roll.

1.

2.

3.

4.

5.

NAME ____________________

Check What You Learned

Adding and Subtracting to 4 Digits (with renaming)

Add or subtract.

	a	b	c	d	e
1.	23 13 +27	8 36 +45	72 38 +43	20 35 +47	86 93 +10
2.	123 427 +192	86 425 +119	19 87 +425	295 221 +196	425 196 176 +105
3.	4321 +1972	5916 + 432	8764 + 492	4567 +1986	5921 +2053
4.	4321 +1985	4321 + 986	4986 +2045	3096 +1779	4305 + 300
5.	3865 − 974	4321 −2280	9871 −4791	4325 −2554	7964 −2872
6.	8212 −6421	9870 −5380	7653 − 482	4987 − 793	1054 − 662
7.	7298 − 792	9784 −6592	4837 −1955	4954 −2063	3219 −1335
8.	8164 −4273	7918 −3633	4327 − 940	9141 −7051	8642 − 951

CHAPTER 4 POSTTEST

NAME ______________________

Check What You Learned

SHOW YOUR WORK

Adding and Subtracting to 4 Digits (with renaming)

Solve each problem.

9. Jerry has 37 red marbles, 42 blue marbles, 13 black marbles, and 23 yellow marbles. How many marbles does Jerry have?

Jerry has __________ marbles.

10. In the year 1976, Mrs. Lopez was 82 years old. In what year was she born?

Mrs. Lopez was born in __________.

11. Estella is 23 years old, Lydia is 27 years old, Toni is 42 years old, and Mai is 18 years old. What are their combined ages?

Their combined ages equal __________ years.

12. Marty earned 586 dollars one week at his job and 432 dollars the next week. Estimate about how much money Marty earned for both weeks.

Marty earned about __________ dollars for both weeks.

13. Holly needs to make 72 cookies for the school bake sale. She has already made 37 cookies. Estimate about how many more cookies she needs to make.

Holly needs to make about __________ more cookies.

9.

10.

11.

12.

13.

CHAPTER 4 POSTTEST

NAME ______________________________

CHAPTER 5 PRETEST

Check What You Know

Multiplying through 2 Digits by 1 Digit

Multiply.

	a	b	c	d	e	f
1.	2 × 0	5 × 1	4 × 3	0 × 2	5 × 6	3 × 8
2.	7 × 2	9 × 3	8 × 8	6 × 3	4 × 5	5 × 4
3.	6 × 6	3 × 9	1 × 7	5 × 3	2 × 6	2 × 2
4.	3 × 0	4 × 7	6 × 9	4 × 4	5 × 1	2 × 9
5.	7 × 4	3 × 7	2 × 3	4 × 2	9 × 1	6 × 5
6.	20 × 4	14 × 3	29 × 3	32 × 4	96 × 2	81 × 1
7.	46 × 4	72 × 1	61 × 3	70 × 2	52 × 4	13 × 5
8.	21 × 5	15 × 3	31 × 4	90 × 2	56 × 3	43 × 3
9.	18 × 3	22 × 4	31 × 2	54 × 5	59 × 1	15 × 4

NAME ______________________

Check What You Know

SHOW YOUR WORK

Multiplying through 2 Digits by 1 Digit

Solve each problem.

10. John bought four 23-cent stamps. How many cents did John spend on stamps?

The stamps cost __________ cents.

10.

11. A clown had 13 balloons that he sold at a carnival for 5 cents each. If he sold all 13 balloons, how much money did he make?

The clown made __________ cents.

11.

12. The movie rental store charges 3 dollars to rent each movie. Miss Padilla rents 5 movies. How much will the movie rental store charge her?

The movie rental store will charge Miss Padilla

__________ dollars.

12.

13. Each semester Henry takes 5 classes. After 8 semesters, how many classes did Henry take?

Henry took __________ classes.

13.

14. Sally wants to buy 3 stickers. The stickers each cost 25 cents. How much will Sally spend on the 3 stickers?

Sally will spend __________ cents on the 3 stickers.

14.

NAME ____________________

Lesson 5.1 Understanding Multiplication

two times seven

2 × 7 means 7 + 7

7	factor	7	
× 2	factor	+ 7	
14	product	14	

five times three

5 × 3 means 5 + 5 + 5

		5
5	factor	5
× 3	factor	+ 5
15	product	15

Multiply. Write the corresponding addition problem next to each multiplication problem.

	a		b	c	d	e
1.	3 × 2 = 6	3 + 3 = 6	7 × 2	6 × 2	9 × 2	8 × 2
2.	2 × 2		1 × 2	5 × 3	6 × 3	3 × 3
3.	2 × 3		1 × 3	4 × 3	7 × 3	2 × 4
4.	4 × 4		1 × 4	5 × 4	9 × 4	8 × 4
5.	3 × 4		4 × 2	5 × 2	8 × 3	9 × 3
6.	6 × 4		7 × 4	3 × 2	7 × 3	9 × 2

NAME ______________________

Lesson 5.2 Multiplying through 5 × 9

factor	3	→	Find the **3**-row.
factor	× 7	→	Find the **7**-column.
product	21	←	The product is named where the 3-row and the 7-column meet.

7-column ↓

3-row →

×	0	1	2	3	4	5	6	7	8	9
0	0	0	0	0	0	0	0	0	0	0
1	0	1	2	3	4	5	6	7	8	9
2	0	2	4	6	8	10	12	14	16	18
3	0	3	6	9	12	15	18	21	24	27
4	0	4	8	12	16	20	24	28	32	36
5	0	5	10	15	20	25	30	35	40	45
6	0	6	12	18	24	30				
7	0	7	14	21	28	35				
8	0	8	16	24	32	40				
9	0	9	18	27	36	45				

Multiply.

	a	b	c	d	e	f
1.	5 ×0 0	3 ×9	6 ×5	1 ×4	5 ×1	6 ×3
2.	9 ×2	8 ×5	5 ×8	0 ×0	2 ×9	3 ×4
3.	4 ×6	7 ×3	6 ×1	7 ×2	3 ×5	4 ×1
4.	6 ×2	5 ×5	9 ×1	2 ×4	3 ×7	7 ×0
5.	0 ×9	3 ×6	7 ×5	5 ×6	3 ×2	4 ×2
6.	7 ×4	3 ×3	1 ×9	2 ×7	0 ×6	1 ×3

NAME ______________________

Lesson 5.3 Multiplying through 9 × 9

factor	6	→	Find the **6**-row.
factor	× 8	→	Find the **8**-column.
product	48	←	The product is named where the 6-row and the 8-column meet.

8-column

6-row

x	0	1	2	3	4	5	6	7	8	9
0	0	0	0	0	0	0	0	0	0	0
1	0	1	2	3	4	5	6	7	8	9
2	0	2	4	6	8	10	12	14	16	18
3	0	3	6	9	12	15	18	21	24	27
4	0	4	8	12	16	20	24	28	32	36
5	0	5	10	15	20	25	30	35	40	45
6	0	6	12	18	24	30	36	42	48	54
7	0	7	14	21	28	35	42	49	56	63
8	0	8	16	24	32	40	48	56	64	72
9	0	9	18	27	36	45	54	63	72	81

Multiply.

	a	b	c	d	e	f
1.	3 × 9 = 27	7 × 6	5 × 4	7 × 9	8 × 6	5 × 0
2.	4 × 3	8 × 5	4 × 9	3 × 0	5 × 7	2 × 9
3.	5 × 1	4 × 6	8 × 2	6 × 8	4 × 0	0 × 9
4.	3 × 1	6 × 4	9 × 2	3 × 4	6 × 3	5 × 6
5.	3 × 8	3 × 6	7 × 6	9 × 9	8 × 4	5 × 3
6.	2 × 6	8 × 8	9 × 3	7 × 4	8 × 0	7 × 7

NAME ______________________

Lesson 5.3 Problem Solving

SHOW YOUR WORK

Solve each problem.

1. Steven wants to buy 6 pieces of bubblegum. Each piece costs 5 cents. How much will he have to pay for the bubblegum?

Steven wants to buy __________ pieces of bubblegum.

One piece of bubblegum costs __________ cents.

Steven will have to pay __________ cents total.

2. There are 7 girls on stage. Each girl is holding 9 flowers. How many flowers are there in all?

There are __________ girls.

Each girl is holding __________ flowers.

There are __________ flowers in all.

3. There are 4 rows of desks. There are 8 desks in each row. How many desks are there in all?

There are __________ rows of desks.

There are __________ desks in each row.

There are __________ desks in all.

4. Sara earns 4 dollars a day babysitting her cousin. If Sara babysits for 5 days, how much money will she earn?

Sara will earn __________ dollars.

5. Jose made 4 points in each of the basketball game's 4 quarters. How many points did he make by the end of the game?

He made a total of __________ points.

1.

2.

3.

4.

5.

NAME ____________________

Lesson 5.4 Multiplying 2 Digits by 1 Digit

	Multiply 2 ones by 3.	Multiply 8 tens by 3.		
$\begin{array}{r} 82 \\ \times\ 3 \\ \hline \end{array}$	$\begin{array}{r} 82 \\ \times\ 3 \\ \hline 6 \end{array}$	$\begin{array}{r} 82 \\ \times\ 3 \\ \hline 6 \\ 240 \end{array}$	$\begin{array}{r} 82 \\ \times\ 3 \\ \hline 6 \\ +240 \\ \hline 246 \end{array}$	← factor ← factor } Add. product

Multiply.

	a	b	c	d	e	f
1.	$\begin{array}{r} 73 \\ \times\ 2 \\ \hline 6 \\ +140 \\ \hline 146 \end{array}$	$\begin{array}{r} 14 \\ \times\ 2 \\ \hline \end{array}$	$\begin{array}{r} 90 \\ \times\ 5 \\ \hline \end{array}$	$\begin{array}{r} 45 \\ \times\ 1 \\ \hline \end{array}$	$\begin{array}{r} 33 \\ \times\ 3 \\ \hline \end{array}$	$\begin{array}{r} 62 \\ \times\ 3 \\ \hline \end{array}$
2.	$\begin{array}{r} 22 \\ \times\ 4 \\ \hline \end{array}$	$\begin{array}{r} 86 \\ \times\ 1 \\ \hline \end{array}$	$\begin{array}{r} 52 \\ \times\ 4 \\ \hline \end{array}$	$\begin{array}{r} 31 \\ \times\ 5 \\ \hline \end{array}$	$\begin{array}{r} 46 \\ \times\ 1 \\ \hline \end{array}$	$\begin{array}{r} 32 \\ \times\ 4 \\ \hline \end{array}$
3.	$\begin{array}{r} 19 \\ \times\ 1 \\ \hline \end{array}$	$\begin{array}{r} 21 \\ \times\ 4 \\ \hline \end{array}$	$\begin{array}{r} 43 \\ \times\ 3 \\ \hline \end{array}$	$\begin{array}{r} 27 \\ \times\ 1 \\ \hline \end{array}$	$\begin{array}{r} 91 \\ \times\ 5 \\ \hline \end{array}$	$\begin{array}{r} 83 \\ \times\ 2 \\ \hline \end{array}$
4.	$\begin{array}{r} 56 \\ \times\ 1 \\ \hline \end{array}$	$\begin{array}{r} 52 \\ \times\ 2 \\ \hline \end{array}$	$\begin{array}{r} 63 \\ \times\ 3 \\ \hline \end{array}$	$\begin{array}{r} 73 \\ \times\ 1 \\ \hline \end{array}$	$\begin{array}{r} 62 \\ \times\ 2 \\ \hline \end{array}$	$\begin{array}{r} 35 \\ \times\ 1 \\ \hline \end{array}$

NAME ______________________

Lesson 5.4 Multiplication Practice

Multiply 2 ones by 4. Multiply 7 tens by 4.

$\begin{array}{r} 72 \\ \times\ 4 \\ \hline \end{array}$	$\begin{array}{r} 72 \\ \times\ 4 \\ \hline 8 \end{array}$	$\begin{array}{r} 72 \\ \times\ 4 \\ \hline 288 \end{array}$

Multiply.

	a	b	c	d	e	f
1.	31 × 5	42 × 2	36 × 1	52 × 4	83 × 3	75 × 1
2.	39 × 1	41 × 4	52 × 2	28 × 1	13 × 3	30 × 5
3.	54 × 2	17 × 1	29 × 0	23 × 3	42 × 4	41 × 5
4.	61 × 5	72 × 3	14 × 2	86 × 1	47 × 1	92 × 3
5.	83 × 2	42 × 3	69 × 3	11 × 5	61 × 2	58 × 1
6.	13 × 2	10 × 5	23 × 2	42 × 1	82 × 4	31 × 4
7.	22 × 3	33 × 2	43 × 3	52 × 3	92 × 2	54 × 1

NAME ______________________

Lesson 5.5 Multiply 2 Digits by 1 Digit (with renaming)

Multiply 6 ones by 3.

$$\begin{array}{r} 26 \\ \times\ 3 \\ \hline \end{array} \qquad \begin{array}{r} ^{1}\ \ \\ 26 \\ \times\ 3 \\ \hline 8 \end{array}$$

$3 \times 6 = 18 = 10 + 8$

Multiply 2 tens by 3. Add the 1 ten.

$3 \times 20 = 60$

$$\begin{array}{r} ^{1}\ \ \\ 26 \\ \times\ 3 \\ \hline 78 \end{array}$$

$60 + 10 = 70$

$$\begin{array}{rl} 26 & \leftarrow \text{factor} \\ \times\ 3 & \leftarrow \text{factor} \\ \hline 78 & \leftarrow \text{product} \end{array}$$

Multiply.

	a	b	c	d	e	f
1.	37 × 2 = 74	19 × 5	45 × 2	38 × 2	25 × 3	12 × 5
2.	14 × 4	47 × 2	28 × 3	13 × 4	23 × 4	24 × 4
3.	26 × 2	36 × 2	13 × 5	15 × 3	27 × 2	18 × 5
4.	15 × 5	17 × 3	24 × 3	39 × 2	14 × 5	16 × 2
5.	27 × 3	15 × 4	29 × 2	26 × 3	36 × 2	17 × 5
6.	35 × 2	25 × 2	28 × 2	14 × 3	17 × 4	29 × 3

NAME ______________________

Lesson 5.5 Multiplying 2 Digits by 1 Digit (with renaming)

Multiply 9 ones by 5.

Multiply 6 tens by 5. Add the 4 tens.

$$\begin{array}{r} 69 \\ \times\ 5 \\ \hline \end{array} \qquad \begin{array}{r} {}^{4}\ \\ 69 \\ \times\ 5 \\ \hline 5 \end{array} \qquad \begin{array}{r} {}^{4}\ \\ 69 \\ \times\ 5 \\ \hline 345 \end{array}$$

$5 \times 9 = 45 = 40 + 5$

$5 \times 60 = 300$

69 ← factor
5 ← factor
345 ← product

$300 + 40 = 340 = 300 + 40$

Multiply.

	a	b	c	d	e	f
1.	72×5 = 360	38×4	29×5	27×4	25×5	36×4
2.	54×3	96×3	84×4	92×5	47×3	86×2
3.	45×3	23×5	86×3	73×5	22×5	56×4
4.	64×3	93×4	86×5	43×4	38×3	74×4
5.	34×3	28×5	37×3	46×4	23×5	83×4
6.	44×3	59×3	82×5	74×5	63×4	47×4

NAME ____________________

Lesson 5.6 Multiplication Practice

Multiply.

	a	b	c	d	e	f
1.	13 × 5	7 × 2	10 × 0	81 × 4	42 × 2	13 × 4
2.	52 × 3	76 × 5	41 × 5	3 × 2	14 × 3	17 × 5
3.	45 × 5	93 × 3	42 × 3	33 × 2	10 × 5	4 × 8
4.	51 × 2	91 × 1	17 × 5	31 × 2	25 × 5	30 × 4
5.	32 × 5	8 × 7	5 × 9	4 × 0	38 × 1	72 × 4
6.	6 × 9	4 × 7	22 × 1	19 × 3	83 × 2	54 × 5
7.	6 × 5	53 × 3	18 × 4	8 × 6	13 × 2	17 × 4
8.	7 × 4	5 × 0	3 × 2	8 × 2	56 × 2	19 × 3
9.	46 × 3	43 × 3	27 × 2	18 × 5	5 × 4	13 × 3

NAME ____________________

Lesson 5.6 Problem Solving

SHOW YOUR WORK

Solve each problem.

1. Gary read 3 books with 56 pages each. How many pages did he read in all?

There are ________ pages in each book.

Gary read ________ books.

Gary read ________ pages in all.

2. There are 5 classes at a school. Each class has 32 students. How many students are at the school?

There are ________ students in each class.

There are ________ classes.

There are ________ students in the school.

3. Yolanda used up 4 rolls of film. If each roll has 24 pictures, how many pictures did she take in all?

Each roll has ________ pictures.

Yolanda used ________ rolls of film.

Yolanda took a total of ________ pictures.

4. During a football game, 2 teams play against each other. There are 11 football players on the field for each team. How many football players are on the field during a football game?

There are ________ football players on the field.

5. There are 12 eggs in a carton of eggs. If Mary buys 6 egg cartons, how many eggs does she have?

Mary has ________ eggs.

1.

2.

3.

4.

5.

NAME ____________________

Check What You Learned

Multiplying through 2 Digits by 1 Digit

Multiply.

	a	b	c	d	e	f
1.	1×5	9×9	3×2	5×4	6×3	8×0
2.	9×7	5×2	6×1	8×2	5×7	3×4
3.	6×5	8×3	4×3	0×8	6×2	4×7
4.	13×2	23×4	17×5	42×1	18×0	23×0
5.	54×2	96×2	53×3	33×2	11×5	40×3
6.	71×2	18×3	20×5	14×3	27×1	19×2
7.	29×3	54×5	21×4	23×4	13×5	12×3
8.	20×4	93×2	17×4	15×3	31×3	21×3
9.	22×3	42×3	11×4	32×5	18×5	95×5

CHAPTER 5 POSTTEST

NAME ____________________

Check What You Learned

SHOW YOUR WORK

Multiplying through 2 Digits by 1 Digit

Solve each problem.

10. Kiri has 5 friends. She gave each friend 3 apples. How many apples did Kiri have?

Kiri had ________ apples.

10.

11. Each of Mr. Black's 4 daughters needs new shoes. Each pair of shoes will cost 29 dollars. How much money will Mr. Black spend on all 4 pairs of shoes?

Mr. Black will spend ________ dollars on the 4 pairs of shoes.

11.

CHAPTER 5 POSTTEST

12. There are 30 students in each classroom. If there are 5 classrooms, how many total students are there?

There are a total of ________ students.

12.

13. There are 7 friends that each have 2 dollars. How much money do the 7 friends have?

The friends have a total of ________ dollars.

13.

14. There is a total of 33 students in Ms. Walker's class. If each student receives 4 papers, how many papers are there?

There are ________ papers in all.

14.

NAME ____________________

CHAPTER 6 PRETEST

Check What You Know

Division Facts through 81 ÷ 9

Divide.

	a	b	c	d	e
1.	4)36	6)54	4)8	8)16	2)12
2.	6)18	9)81	4)4	6)30	3)9
3.	7)14	3)21	5)40	3)24	4)16
4.	1)5	3)6	5)10	4)12	5)30
5.	7)49	9)63	4)32	2)14	1)8
6.	5)20	1)8	7)7	3)27	5)35
7.	8)40	7)21	9)45	7)42	8)64
8.	2)18	3)15	6)12	6)24	8)48
9.	6)6	2)8	9)36	4)20	2)16

NAME ________________

CHAPTER 6 PRETEST

Check What You Know

Division Facts through 81 ÷ 9

SHOW YOUR WORK

Solve each problem.

10. There are 36 students who live in the college dormitory. If 4 students live in each room, how many rooms are there in the dormitory?

There are ________ rooms in the dormitory.

11. A package of 42 candies is evenly divided among 7 people. How many candies does each person receive?

Each person receives ________ candies.

12. A bookshelf contains 56 books. There are 7 shelves in the bookshelf. Each shelf has the same number of books on it. How many books are on each shelf?

There are ________ books on each shelf.

13. Eight people paid a total of 24 dollars for admission into the school carnival. If each ticket cost the same amount, how much did each ticket cost?

The cost of each ticket was ________ dollars.

14. A family of 5 takes an ice chest to the beach. There are 10 water bottles in the ice chest. How many water bottles will each person receive if each person receives the same number of water bottles?

Each person will receive ________ water bottles.

15. Eighteen fish were caught on a deep-sea fishing boat. If each person on the boat caught 2 fish, how many people were on the boat?

There were ________ people on the boat.

10.

11.

12.

13.

14.

15.

NAME ______________________________

Lesson 6.1 Understanding Division

$\overline{)}$ means divide.

divisor ⟶ $\begin{array}{r}6\\3\overline{)18}\end{array}$ ⟵ quotient (6) ⟵ dividend (18)

$\begin{array}{r}6\\3\overline{)18}\end{array}$ is read "18 divided by 3 is equal to 6."

$\begin{array}{r}3\\4\overline{)12}\end{array}$ is read "12 divided by 4 is equal to 3."

In $\begin{array}{r}3\\4\overline{)12}\end{array}$, the divisor is 4, the dividend is 12, and the quotient is 3.

÷ also means divide.

$10 \div 2 = 5$

dividend (10) divisor (2) quotient (5)

$10 \div 2 = 5$ is read "10 divided by 2 is equal to 5."

$6 \div 3 = 2$ is read "6 divided by 3 is equal to 2."

In $6 \div 3 = 2$, the divisor is 3, the dividend is 6, and the quotient is 2.

Complete each sentence.

1. $\begin{array}{r}2\\6\overline{)12}\end{array}$ is read "<u>12</u> divided by 6 is equal to <u>2</u>."
2. $\begin{array}{r}3\\8\overline{)24}\end{array}$ is read "____ divided by 8 is equal to ____."
3. $\begin{array}{r}9\\4\overline{)36}\end{array}$ is read "____ divided by 4 is equal to ____."
4. In $\begin{array}{r}2\\4\overline{)8}\end{array}$, the divisor is ____, the dividend is ____, and the quotient is ____.
5. In $\begin{array}{r}5\\7\overline{)35}\end{array}$, the divisor is ____, the dividend is ____, and the quotient is ____.
6. $20 \div 5 = 4$ is read "____ divided by 5 is equal to ____."
7. $27 \div 9 = 3$ is read "____ divided by 9 is equal to ____."
8. $6 \div 2 = 3$ is read "____ divided by 2 is equal to ____."
9. In $15 \div 3 = 5$, the divisor is ____, the dividend is ____, and the quotient is ____.
10. In $14 \div 2 = 7$, the divisor is ____, the dividend is ____, and the quotient is ____.

NAME ____________________

Lesson 6.1 Understanding Division

8 △ in all.
4 △ in each group.
How many groups?
8 ÷ 4 = 2
There are 2 groups.

△△△△
△△△△

8 △ in all.
2 groups of △.
How many △ in each group?
8 ÷ 2 = 4
There are 4 in each group.

Check by multiplication: quotient × divisor = dividend.

2 × 4 = 8 4 × 2 = 8

Complete the following.

a

1. 12 □ in all.
3 □ in each group.
How many groups?
12 ÷ 3 = 4
There are 4 groups.
Check: 4 × 3 = 12

□□□
□□□
□□□
□□□

b

12 □ in all.
4 groups of □.
How many in each group?
12 ÷ 4 = ______
There are ______ □ in each group.
Check: ______________

2. 20 As in all.
______ As in each group.
How many groups?
20 ÷ 4 = ______
There are ______ groups.
Check: ______________

AAAA
AAAA
AAAA
AAAA
AAAA

20 As in all.
______ groups of As.
How many in each group?
20 ÷ 5 = ______
There are ______ As in each group.
Check: ______________

3. ______ Fs in all.
______ Fs in each group.
How many groups?
12 ÷ 2 = ______
There are ______ groups.
Check: ______________

FF
FF
FF
FF
FF
FF

______ Fs in all.
______ groups of Fs.
How many in each group?
12 ÷ 6 = ______
There are ______ Fs in each group.
Check: ______________

NAME ____________________

Lesson 6.2 Dividing through 27 ÷ 3

$$\begin{array}{r} 5 \\ \times\ 3 \\ \hline 15 \end{array} \quad \longrightarrow \quad 3\overline{)15}^{\,5}$$

If 3 × 5 = 15, then 15 ÷ 3 = 5.

$$\begin{array}{r} 6 \\ \times\ 2 \\ \hline 12 \end{array} \quad \longrightarrow \quad 2\overline{)12}^{\,6}$$

If 2 × 6 = 12, then 12 ÷ 2 = 6.

Divide. Under each division problem, write the corresponding multiplication problem.

	a	b	c	d	e
1.	3)6 = 2 3 × 2 = 6	2)14 = 7 2 × 7 = 14	1)5	2)4	1)4
2.	3)27	1)3	2)18	1)7	3)21
3.	3)12	2)16	1)5	3)18	2)10
4.	1)6	1)8	2)8	1)2	1)1
5.	3)24	3)9	1)9	2)6	2)2

NAME ____________________

Lesson 6.2 Problem Solving

SHOW YOUR WORK

Solve each problem.

1. Joe's fish store has 18 goldfish. The fish are in 3 aquariums. The same number of goldfish are in each aquarium. How many goldfish are in each aquarium?

   There are ________ goldfish.

   There are ________ aquariums.

   There are ________ goldfish in each aquarium.

2. Sally has 16 shoes in her closet. A pair of shoes is a group of 2 shoes. How many pairs of shoes does Sally have?

   Sally has ________ shoes.

   A pair is a group of ________ shoes.

   Sally has ________ pairs of shoes.

3. The egg carton has 12 eggs in it. There are 2 rows in the carton. How many eggs are in each row?

   The egg carton has ________ eggs.

   There are ________ rows in the carton.

   There are ________ eggs in each row.

4. Elisa has 15 sticks of gum. If she gives each of her 3 friends the same number of sticks of gum, how many sticks of gum will each of Elisa's friends have?

   Each of Elisa's friends will have ________ sticks of gum.

5. Alvin earned 27 dollars for mowing 3 lawns on Saturday. Alvin earned the same amount of money for each lawn. How much did he earn for each lawn?

   Alvin earned ________ dollars for each lawn he mowed.

1.	
2.	
3.	
4.	5.

NAME ______________________

Lesson 6.3 Dividing through 54 ÷ 6

$$\begin{array}{r} 5 \\ \times\ 4 \\ \hline 20 \end{array} \longrightarrow 4\overline{)20}^{\,5}$$

If 4 × 5 = 20, then 20 ÷ 4 = 5.

$$\begin{array}{r} 8 \\ \times\ 6 \\ \hline 48 \end{array} \longrightarrow 6\overline{)48}^{\,8}$$

If 6 × 8 = 48, then 48 ÷ 6 = 8.

Divide. Under each division problem write the corresponding multiplication problem.

	a	b	c	d	e
1.	9 6)54 6 × 9 = 54	3)27	6)48	5)25	4)36
2.	5)30	4)24	4)32	4)16	4)20

Divide.

	a	b	c	d	e
3.	6)36	4)28	5)35	6)24	3)21
4.	5)45	6)12	5)40	3)24	6)18
5.	3)12	2)16	4)12	2)18	3)9
6.	5)15	6)42	3)18	6)6	3)27

NAME ________________

Lesson 6.3 Problem Solving

SHOW YOUR WORK

Solve each problem.

1. There are 24 hours in a day. If the day is divided into 6 equal time segments, how many hours will be in each time segment?

There are ________ hours.

There are ________ time segments.

There are ________ hours in each time segment.

2. There are 30 desks in the classroom. There are 6 desks in each row. How many rows of desks are there?

There are ________ desks.

There are ________ desks in each row.

There are ________ rows of desks.

3. Mr. Villa handed out 42 papers to 6 students. Each student received the same number of papers. How many papers did each student receive?

Mr. Villa handed out ________ papers.

There are ________ students.

Each student received ________ papers.

4. There are 12 months in a year. There are 4 seasons in a year. If each season has an equal number of months, how many months are in each season?

There are ________ months in each season.

5. Bianca has 48 roses. She has 6 vases. Bianca wants to put an equal number of roses in each vase. How many roses will Bianca put in each vase?

Bianca will put ________ roses in each vase.

1.

2.

3.

4.

5.

NAME ______________________

Lesson 6.4 Dividing through 81 ÷ 9

$$\begin{array}{r} 6 \\ \times\ 9 \\ \hline 54 \end{array} \longrightarrow 9\overline{)54} = 6$$

If 9 × 6 = 54, then 54 ÷ 9 = 6.

$$\begin{array}{r} 9 \\ \times\ 7 \\ \hline 63 \end{array} \longrightarrow 7\overline{)63} = 9$$

If 7 × 9 = 63, then 63 ÷ 7 = 9.

Divide. Under each division problem write the corresponding multiplication problem.

	a	b	c	d	e
1.	$7\overline{)7}$ = 1 7 × 1 = 7	$6\overline{)24}$	$8\overline{)56}$	$6\overline{)30}$	$8\overline{)64}$
2.	$6\overline{)12}$	$7\overline{)35}$	$8\overline{)24}$	$7\overline{)28}$	$6\overline{)36}$

Divide.

	a	b	c	d	e
3.	$9\overline{)63}$	$9\overline{)81}$	$7\overline{)56}$	$5\overline{)35}$	$8\overline{)24}$
4.	$9\overline{)18}$	$7\overline{)14}$	$7\overline{)21}$	$8\overline{)48}$	$9\overline{)45}$
5.	$7\overline{)49}$	$8\overline{)16}$	$9\overline{)27}$	$9\overline{)9}$	$7\overline{)42}$
6.	$9\overline{)27}$	$9\overline{)54}$	$8\overline{)8}$	$6\overline{)54}$	$8\overline{)40}$

NAME ____________________

Lesson 6.4 Problem Solving

SHOW YOUR WORK

Solve each problem.

1. Spencer wants to save 72 dollars. How many weeks will it take Spencer to save 72 dollars if he saves 9 dollars each week?

Spencer wants to save __________ dollars.

He saves __________ dollars each week.

It will take Spencer __________ weeks to save 72 dollars.

2. Ms. Jefferson worked 40 hours this week. She worked 8 hours each day. How many days did she work this week?

Ms. Jefferson worked __________ hours this week.

She worked __________ hours each day.

She worked __________ days this week.

3. There are 16 football players on the field. If there are 8 players on each team, how many teams are on the field?

There are __________ football players on the field.

There are __________ players on each team.

There are __________ teams on the field.

4. Mrs. Daniels ordered 7 tables and 63 chairs for a banquet. Each table will have the same number of chairs. How many chairs will be at each table?

There will be __________ chairs at each table.

1.

2.

3.

4.

NAME ____________________

Lesson 6.5 Division Practice

Divide.

	a	b	c	d	e
1.	5)25	4)16	7)21	9)81	6)18
2.	6)54	3)27	9)72	7)49	5)5
3.	3)24	4)28	9)36	2)14	1)9
4.	3)6	8)16	7)35	5)15	3)9
5.	7)42	9)45	2)2	7)63	2)6
6.	5)20	2)18	8)32	4)24	8)72
7.	1)1	8)64	6)36	5)45	2)16
8.	8)48	3)15	3)21	9)54	1)5
9.	8)24	7)28	4)36	7)14	9)9
10.	5)35	6)42	5)45	1)2	9)63

NAME ______________________

Lesson 6.6 Division and Multiplication Practice

Divide or multiply.

	a	b	c	d	e	f
1.	$3\overline{)6}$	$9\overline{)18}$	$4\overline{)36}$	$6\overline{)54}$	$3\overline{)27}$	$2\overline{)4}$
2.	$8\overline{)40}$	$3\overline{)18}$	$2\overline{)6}$	$3\overline{)9}$	$2\overline{)16}$	$5\overline{)20}$
3.	$4\overline{)32}$	$9\overline{)27}$	$2\overline{)8}$	$1\overline{)7}$	$5\overline{)5}$	$9\overline{)54}$
4.	$7\overline{)42}$	$6\overline{)12}$	$9\overline{)81}$	$4\overline{)4}$	$6\overline{)24}$	$2\overline{)10}$
5.	$1\overline{)2}$	$4\overline{)20}$	$3\overline{)15}$	$6\overline{)48}$	$3\overline{)12}$	$8\overline{)56}$
6.	86×3	72×5	67×4	91×9	22×7	10×6
7.	51×2	38×7	43×8	29×1	18×6	97×3
8.	7×6	16×9	82×5	33×3	17×8	56×2
9.	13×6	10×7	73×5	64×8	31×9	9×2
10.	53×8	76×4	21×7	89×2	47×5	28×9

NAME ____________________

Check What You Learned

Division Facts through 81 ÷ 9

CHAPTER 6 POSTTEST

Divide.

	a	b	c	d	e
1.	1)‾4	2)‾16	9)‾63	7)‾42	5)‾20
2.	9)‾54	9)‾9	4)‾12	1)‾6	9)‾36
3.	8)‾16	5)‾25	2)‾12	4)‾8	3)‾6
4.	8)‾8	6)‾30	6)‾18	6)‾54	9)‾27
5.	2)‾14	2)‾10	1)‾3	4)‾20	3)‾18
6.	8)‾72	2)‾6	7)‾56	3)‾24	4)‾32
7.	7)‾63	4)‾16	8)‾32	5)‾30	2)‾8
8.	7)‾7	8)‾24	3)‾27	6)‾6	1)‾8
9.	5)‾35	6)‾42	6)‾36	8)‾64	3)‾21

NAME ____________________

Check What You Learned

SHOW YOUR WORK

Division Facts through 81 ÷ 9

Solve each problem.

10. There are 64 pages in a book. There are 8 chapters in the book. Each chapter has the same number of pages. How many pages are in each chapter of the book?

There are __________ pages in each chapter of the book.

11. Six horses can live in the stable. If 1 horse can live in each stall, how many stalls are in the stable?

There are __________ stalls in the stable.

12. A golfer shot a score of 45 in a golf match. She played 9 holes. She had the same score at each of the holes. What was her score at each hole?

She shot a score of __________ at each hole.

13. A package of 12 donuts was shared evenly among 3 friends. How many donuts did each friend receive?

Each friend received __________ donuts.

14. A bicycle has 18 speeds. Each of its 2 gears has the same number of speeds. How many speeds does the bicycle have for each gear?

Each gear has __________ speeds.

15. Forty teenagers went on a river-rafting trip. If each raft held 8 teenagers, how many rafts did the teenagers have for their trip?

The teenagers had __________ rafts.

10.

11.

12.

13.

14.

15.

NAME ____________________

Mid-Test Chapters 1–6

Add or subtract.

	a	b	c	d	e
1.	5 + 3	7 + 12	33 + 2	19 + 7	21 + 5
2.	54 + 13	16 + 42	96 + 39	16 + 54	87 + 63
3.	116 + 23	110 + 30	319 + 400	607 + 401	632 + 481
4.	23 + 39 + 42	11 + 31 + 73	29 + 36 + 5	192 + 305 + 486	611 + 812 + 233
5.	53 − 13	49 − 23	16 − 9	29 − 21	18 − 2
6.	36 − 19	25 − 16	85 − 14	92 − 33	45 − 26
7.	511 − 31	206 − 92	554 − 41	592 − 51	793 − 82
8.	300 − 200	596 − 485	311 − 120	529 − 153	697 − 593

NAME ____________________

Mid-Test Chapters 1–6

Add or subtract.

	a	b	c	d	e
9.	1034 + 311	6654 +2862	5112 +3342	5762 +2903	4863 +2971
10.	7107 +1986	5403 +1969	4321 +2642	1969 +2543	6032 +2961
11.	5110 − 210	8692 − 451	9893 −4541	6103 −5002	3000 −1000
12.	5106 − 320	7980 − 990	6457 −4366	9875 −1994	8764 −3873

Round each number to the place named.

	a	b	c	d	e
13.	5,432 tens	986 tens	78,654 hundreds	9,865 tens	54,329 thousands
	______	______	______	______	______

Write each number in expanded form.

	a	b	c	d
14.	50,462	19,783	543	10,030
	______	______	______	______

Compare each pair of numbers. Write <, >, or =.

	a	b	c	d	e
15.	32 ___ 93	110 ___ 110	54 ___ 52	16 ___ 61	103 ___ 13

NAME ______________________________

Mid-Test Chapters 1–6

Multiply.

	a	b	c	d	e
16.	5×5	6×1	29×5	8×7	6×3
17.	84×3	9×7	6×5	44×2	39×1
18.	7×6	17×3	34×5	53×2	9×8
19.	15×4	62×3	19×3	2×4	23×4

Divide.

	a	b	c	d	e
20.	$6\overline{)18}$	$9\overline{)54}$	$8\overline{)48}$	$4\overline{)8}$	$6\overline{)6}$
21.	$9\overline{)81}$	$9\overline{)63}$	$2\overline{)16}$	$7\overline{)14}$	$6\overline{)36}$
22.	$9\overline{)18}$	$7\overline{)7}$	$6\overline{)12}$	$3\overline{)27}$	$8\overline{)24}$
23.	$3\overline{)21}$	$2\overline{)4}$	$4\overline{)32}$	$1\overline{)5}$	$9\overline{)27}$

CHAPTERS 1–6 MID-TEST

NAME ____________________

Mid-Test Chapters 1–6

SHOW YOUR WORK

Solve each problem.

24. Sarah has 50 marbles and Jessie has 63 marbles. How many marbles do they have together?

Sarah and Jessie have ______ marbles together.

25. A pencil costs 48 cents and a package of gum costs 29 cents. Estimate about how much the pencil and the package of gum cost together.

The pencil and the package of gum cost about

______ cents.

26. Gloria has saved 329 dollars. If she spends 58 dollars, how much money will she have left?

Gloria will have ______ dollars left.

27. Tito read 320 pages in a book. Akando read 323 pages in a book. Kenji read 313 pages in a book. How many pages did they read?

Tito, Akando, and Kenji read ______ pages.

28. In the year 1983, Mr. Smith was 94 years old. In what year was he born?

Mr. Smith was born in the year ______.

29. Tobias gave each of his 7 friends 4 baseball cards. How many baseball cards did Tobias give to his friends?

Tobias gave ______ trading cards to his friends.

30. Thirty-five people want to go camping. If each campsite can have a maximum of 7 people, what is the fewest number of campsites needed?

The least number of campsites needed is ______.

24.	**25.**
26.	**27.**
28.	**29.**
30.	

NAME ______________________

Check What You Know

Fractions

What fraction of each figure is shaded?

1.

a

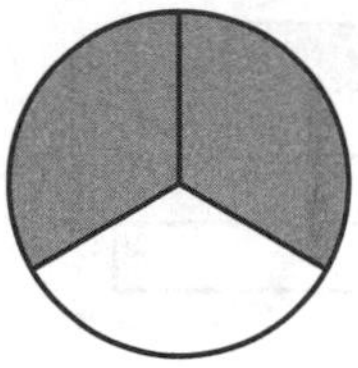

______

b

______

c

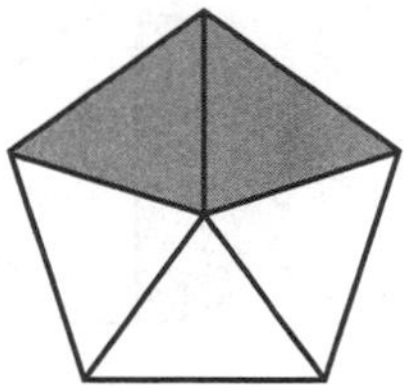

______

2.

a

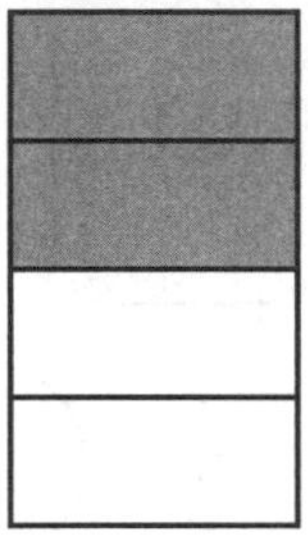

______

b

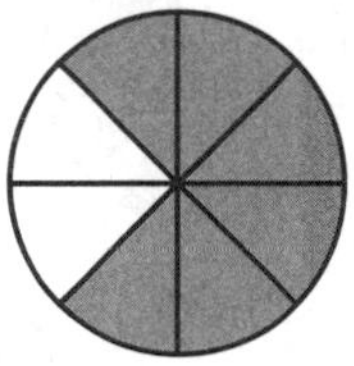

______

c

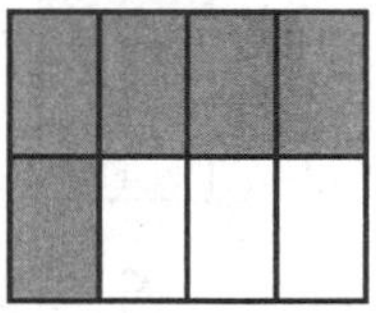

______

What fraction of each set is shaded?

3.

a

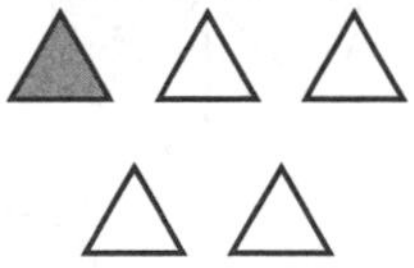

______

b

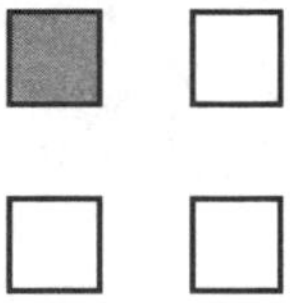

______

c

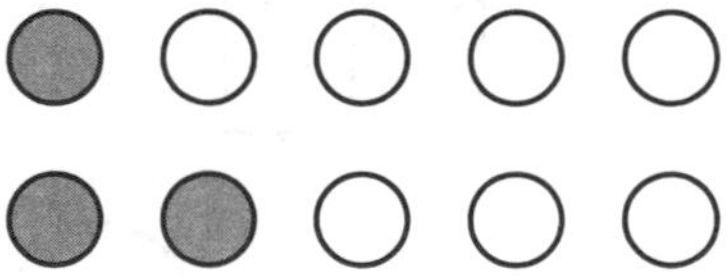

______

4.

a

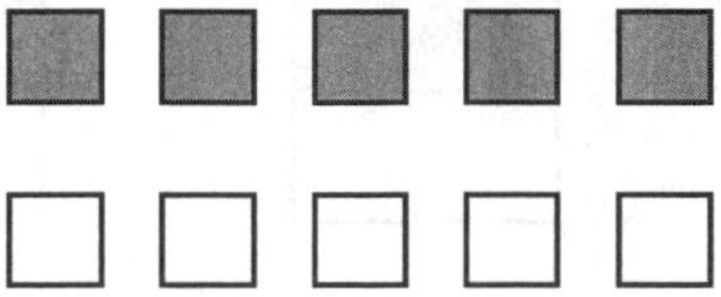

______

b

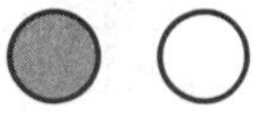

______

c

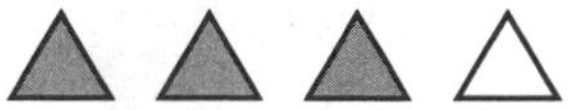

______

NAME ____________________

Check What You Know

Fractions

Use >, <, or = to compare the fractions.

5.

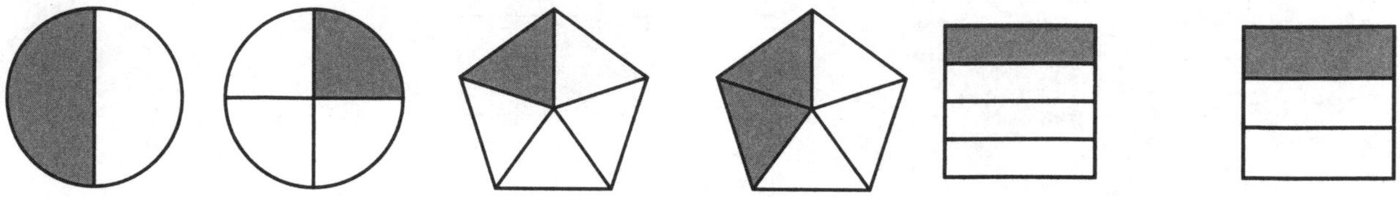

a. $\frac{1}{2}$ ◯ $\frac{1}{4}$ b. $\frac{1}{5}$ ◯ $\frac{2}{5}$ c. $\frac{1}{4}$ ◯ $\frac{1}{3}$

6.

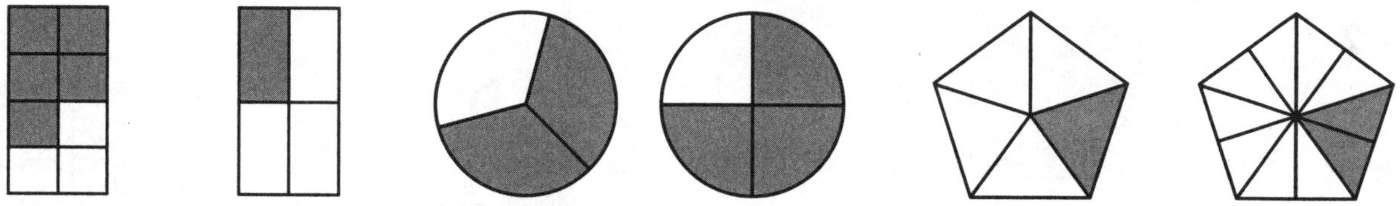

a. $\frac{5}{8}$ ◯ $\frac{1}{4}$ b. $\frac{2}{3}$ ◯ $\frac{3}{4}$ c. $\frac{1}{5}$ ◯ $\frac{2}{10}$

What fraction of each figure is shaded? Compare the fractions. Use >, <, or =.

7.

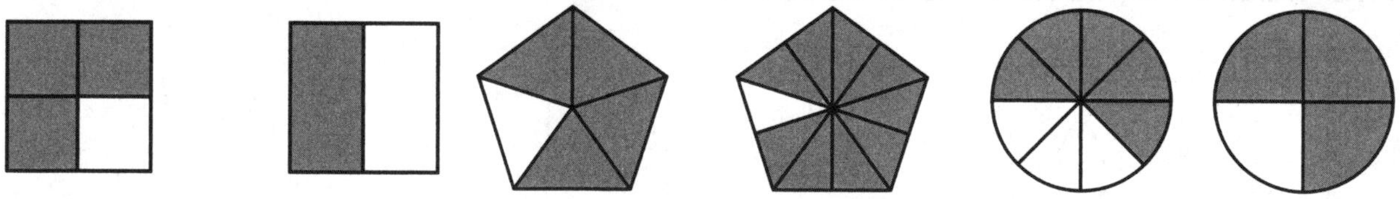

a. _____ ◯ _____ b. _____ ◯ _____ c. _____ ◯ _____

8.

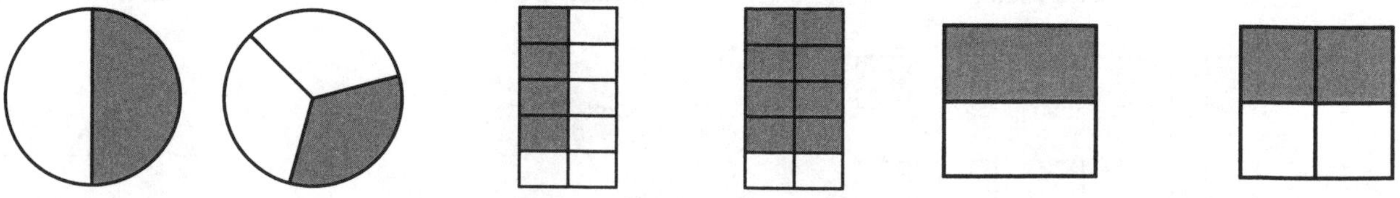

a. _____ ◯ _____ b. _____ ◯ _____ c. _____ ◯ _____

NAME ______________________

Lesson 7.1 Parts of a Whole

A fraction is a number for part of a whole.

$\frac{1}{4}$ ← numerator (part of the whole)
← denominator (parts in all)

1 ← part shaded
4 ← parts in all

$\frac{1}{4}$ of the square is shaded.

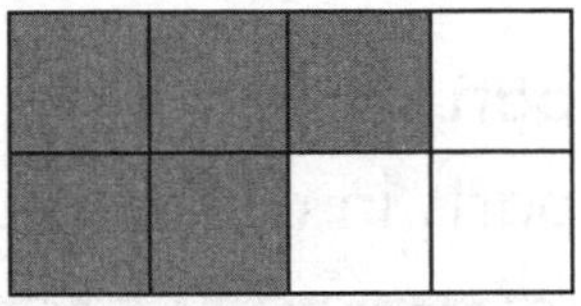

5 ← parts shaded
8 ← parts in all

$\frac{5}{8}$ of the rectangle is shaded.

What fraction of each figure is shaded?

	a	b	c
1.	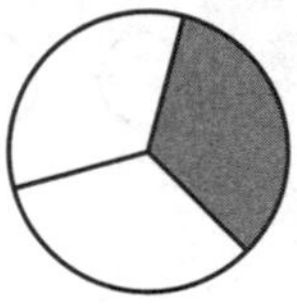 $\frac{1}{3}$	 ______	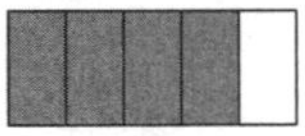 ______
2.	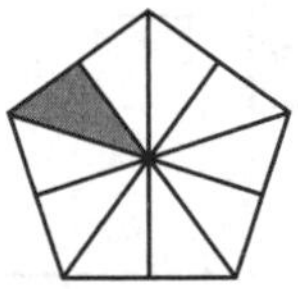 ______	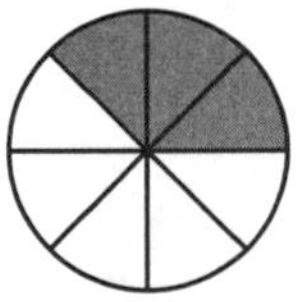 ______	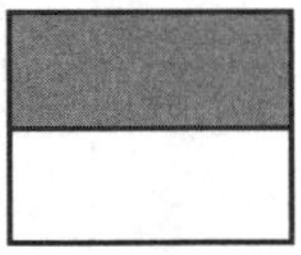 ______
3.	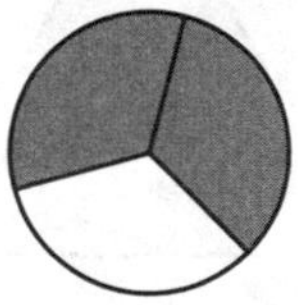 ______	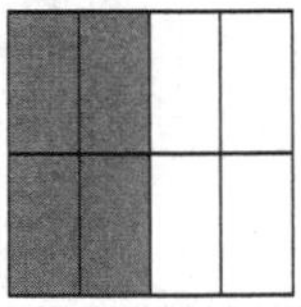 ______	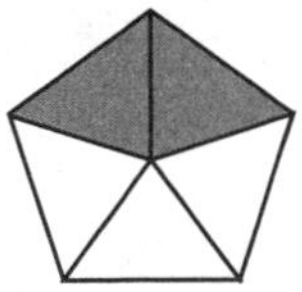 ______
4.	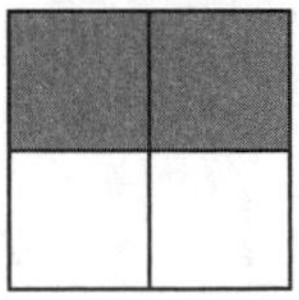 ______	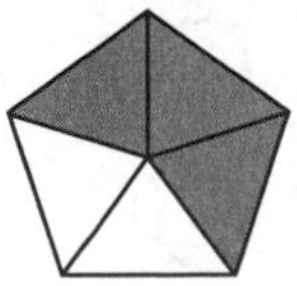 ______	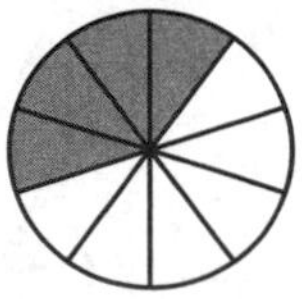 ______

NAME ______________________

Lesson 7.2 Parts of a Set

A fraction is a number for part of a set.

$\frac{1}{2}$ ← numerator (part of the set)
← denominator (parts in all the set)

$\frac{1}{2}$ ← part shaded ← parts in all the set

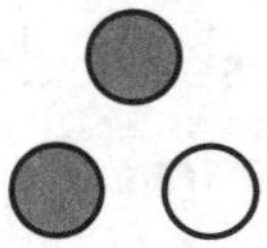

$\frac{2}{3}$ ← parts shaded ← parts in all the set

What fraction of each set is shaded?

1.

a

$\frac{4}{5}$ ________

b

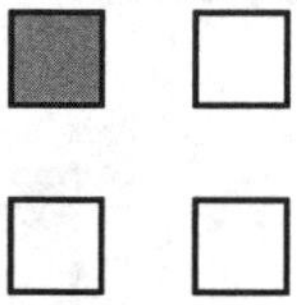

____

c

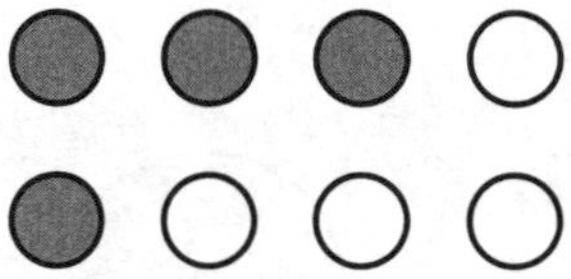

____

2.

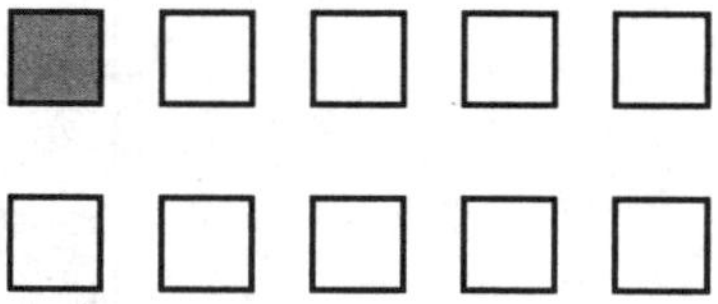

____

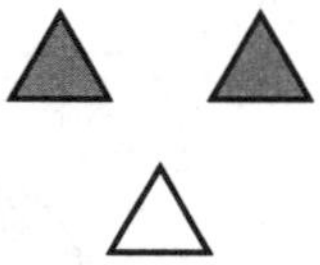

____

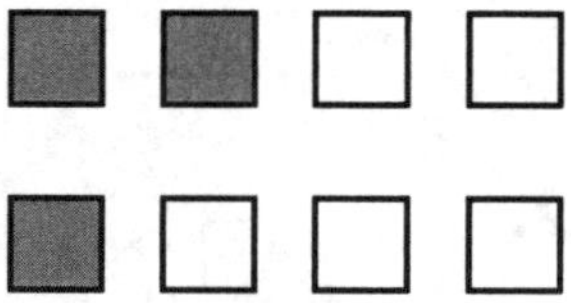

____

3.

____

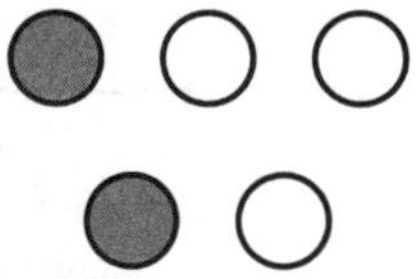

____

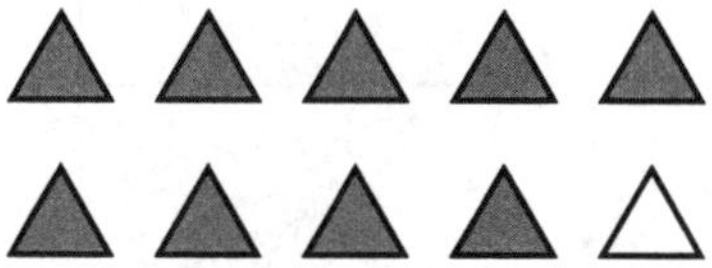

____

Shade the number indicated by the fraction.

4.

a

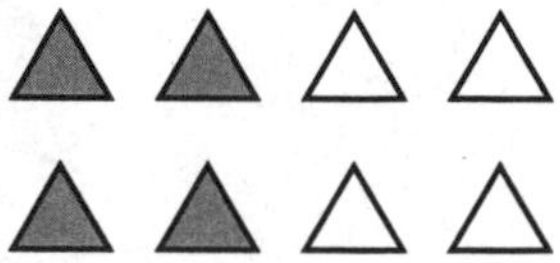

$\frac{4}{8}$

b

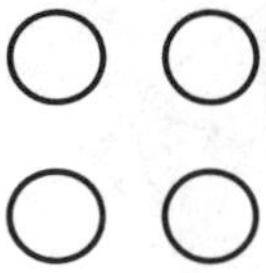

$\frac{3}{4}$

c

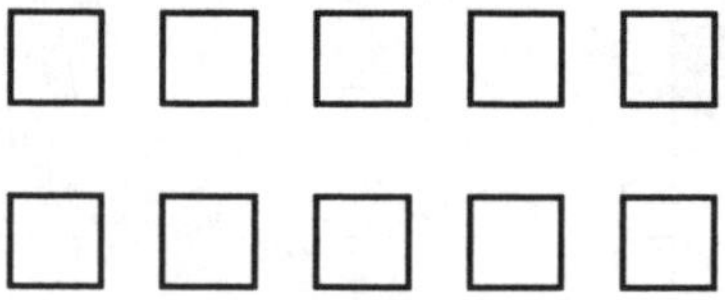

$\frac{3}{10}$

d

$\frac{1}{5}$

NAME ____________________

Lesson 7.3 Comparing Fractions

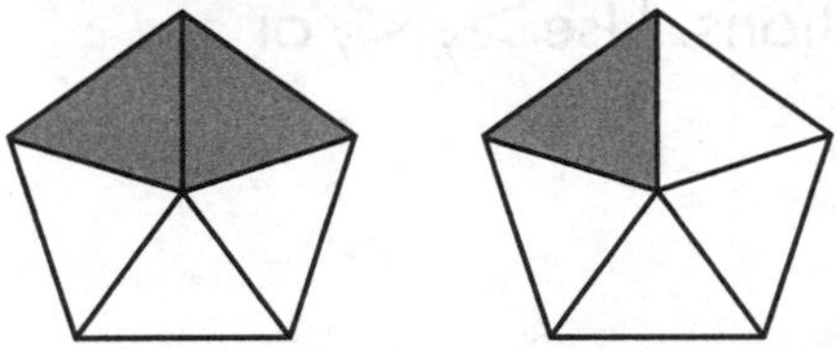 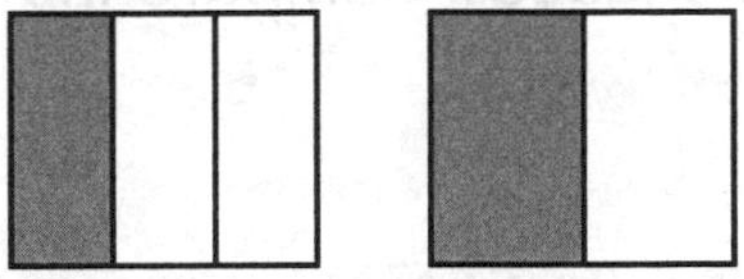 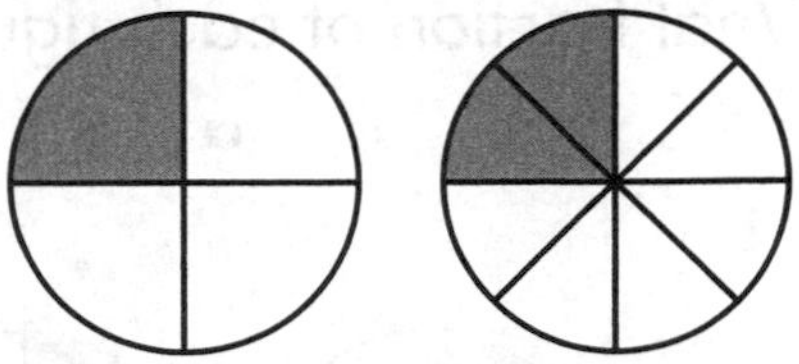

$\frac{2}{5} > \frac{1}{5}$ $\frac{1}{3} < \frac{1}{2}$ $\frac{1}{4} = \frac{2}{8}$

$\frac{2}{5}$ is greater than $\frac{1}{5}$. $\frac{1}{3}$ is less than $\frac{1}{2}$. $\frac{1}{4}$ is equal to $\frac{2}{8}$.

Use >, <, or = to compare the fractions.

	a	b	c
1.	 $\frac{1}{4}$ (<) $\frac{3}{4}$	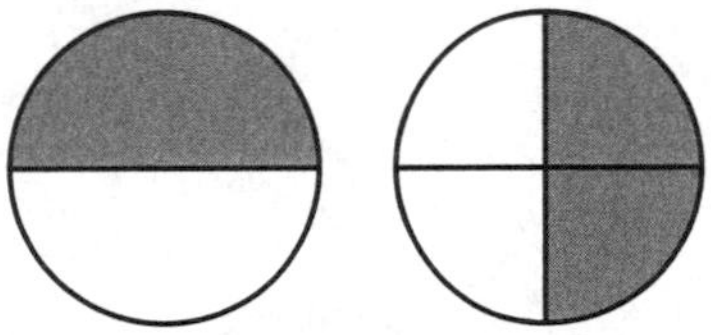 $\frac{1}{2}$ ( ) $\frac{2}{4}$	 $\frac{2}{3}$ ( ) $\frac{1}{2}$
2.	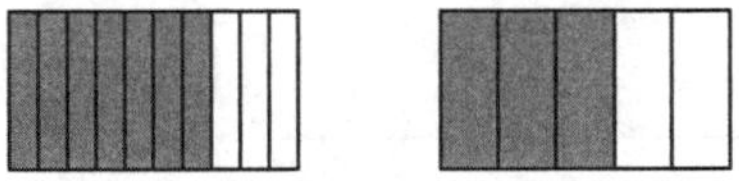 $\frac{7}{10}$ ( ) $\frac{3}{5}$	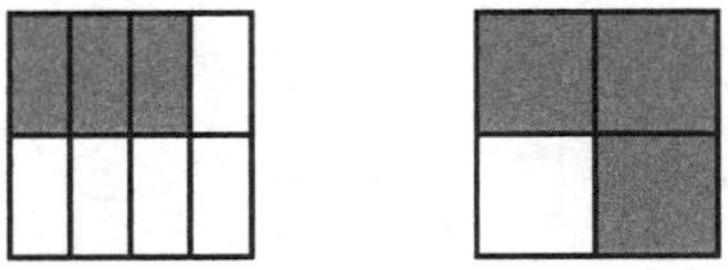 $\frac{3}{8}$ ( ) $\frac{3}{4}$	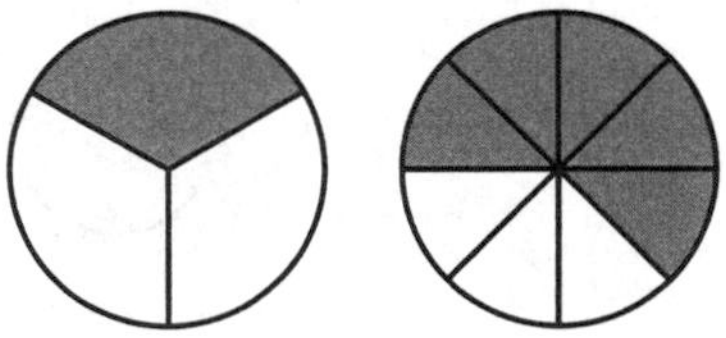 $\frac{1}{3}$ ( ) $\frac{5}{8}$
3.	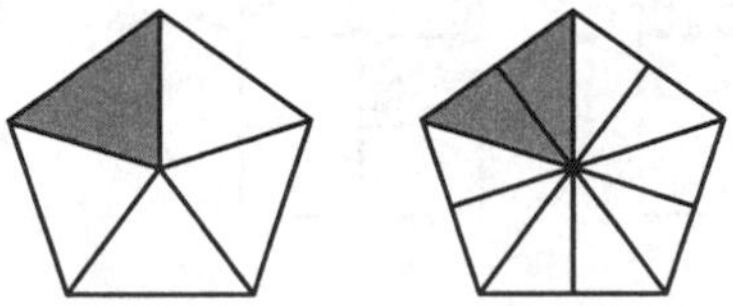 $\frac{1}{5}$ ( ) $\frac{2}{10}$	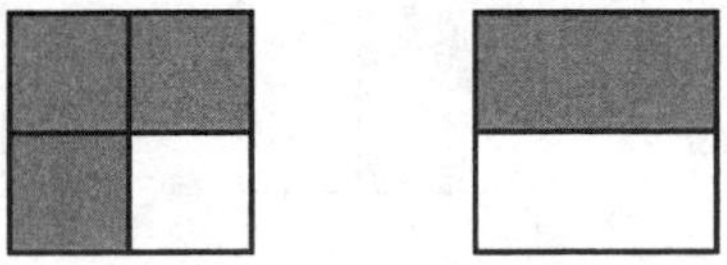 $\frac{3}{4}$ ( ) $\frac{1}{2}$	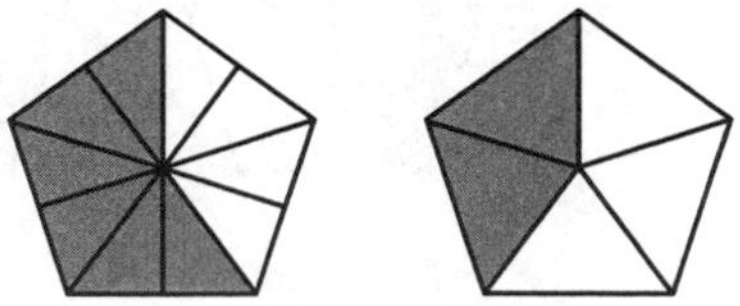 $\frac{6}{10}$ ( ) $\frac{2}{5}$

Lesson 7.3 Comparing Fractions

What fraction of each figure is shaded? Compare the fractions. Use >, <, or = .

1.

a

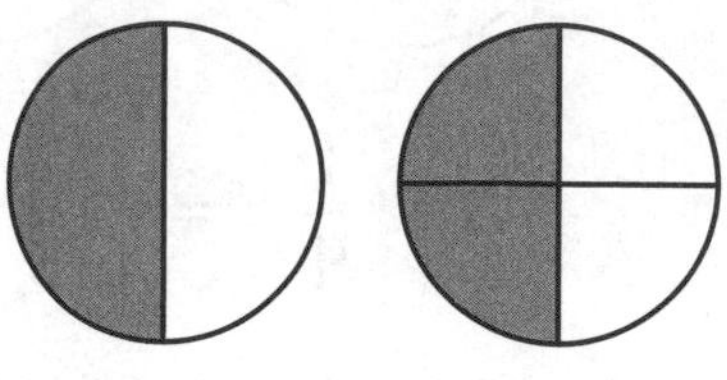

$\frac{1}{2}$ (=) $\frac{2}{4}$

b

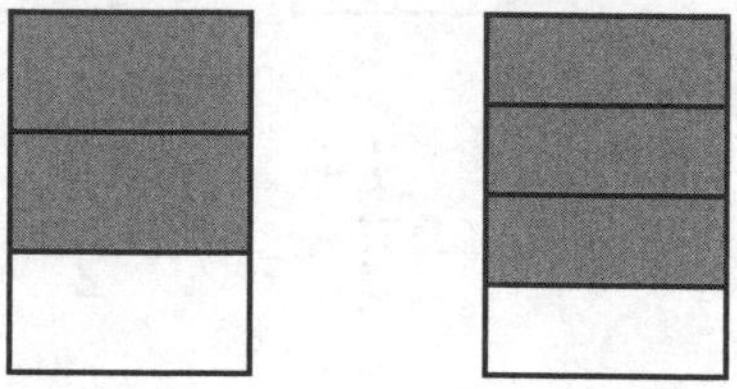

_____ ◯ _____

c

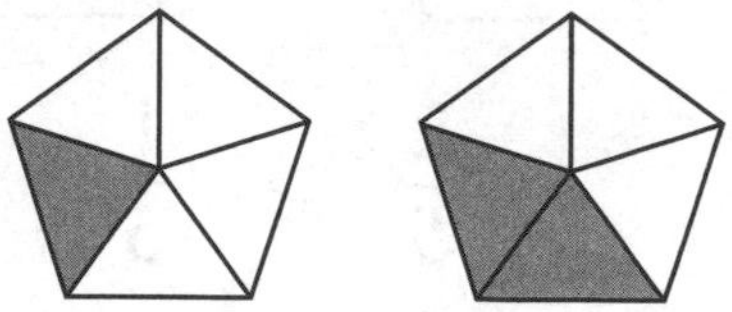

_____ ◯ _____

2.

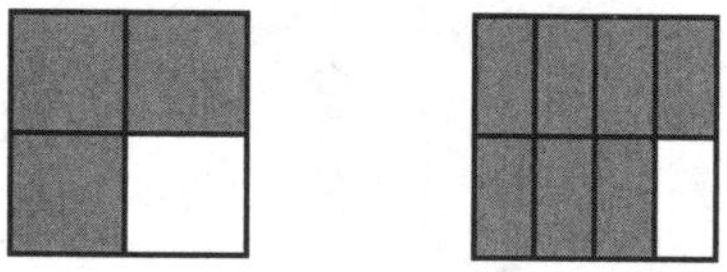

_____ ◯ _____

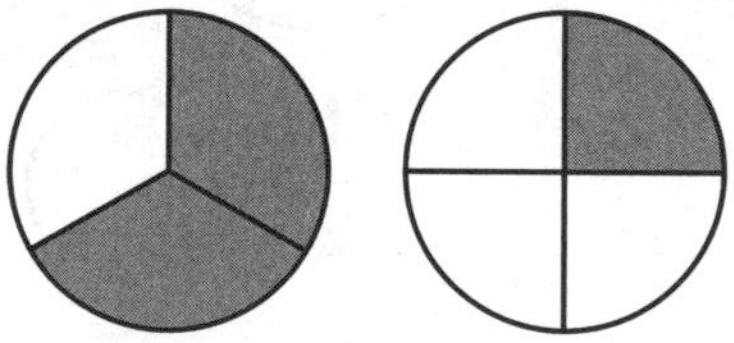

_____ ◯ _____

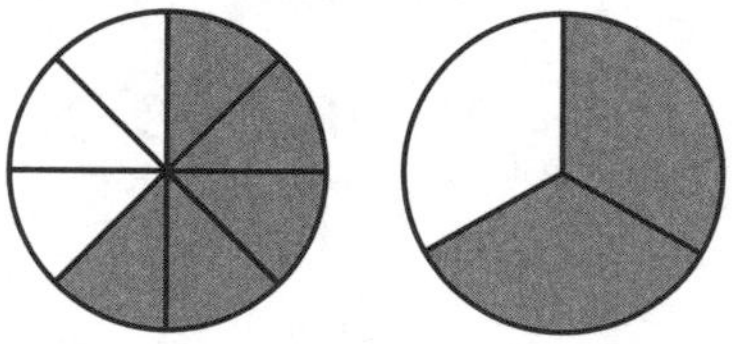

_____ ◯ _____

3.

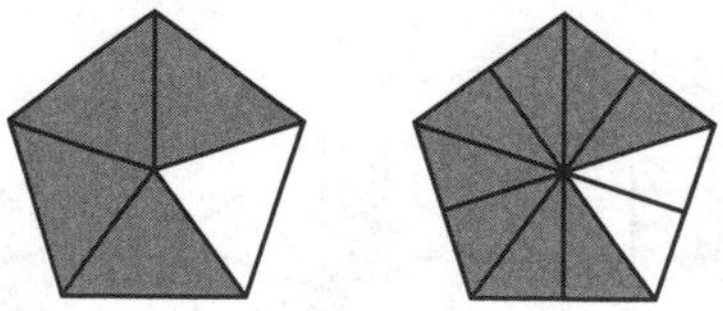

_____ ◯ _____

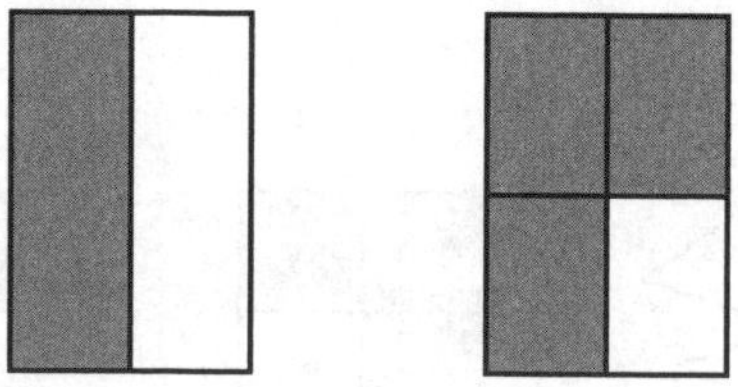

_____ ◯ _____

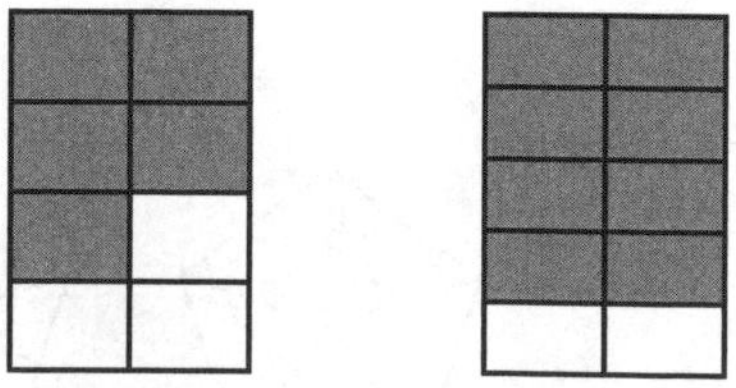

_____ ◯ _____

NAME ______________________

Check What You Learned

Fractions

What fraction of each figure is shaded?

	a	b	c
1.	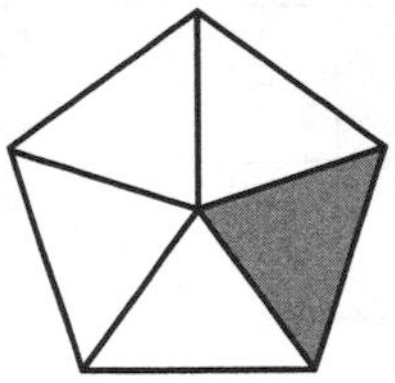	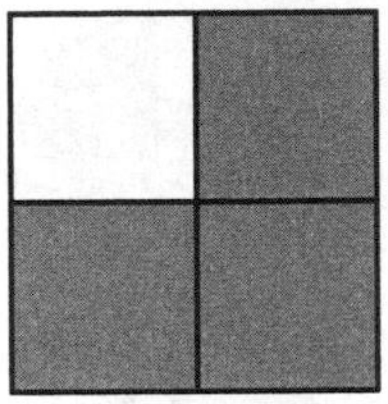	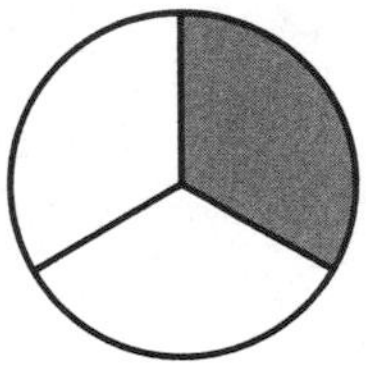
2.	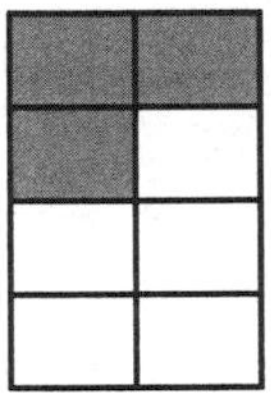	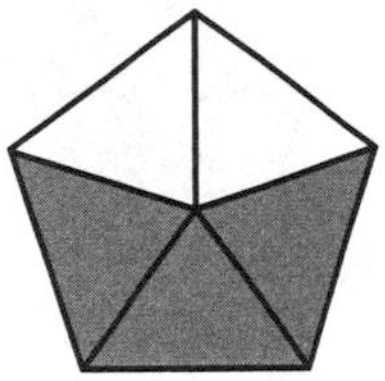	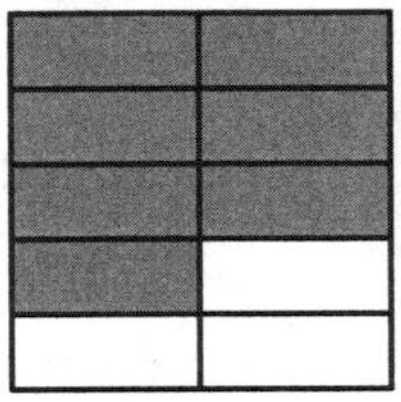

What fraction of each set is shaded?

	a	b	c
3.	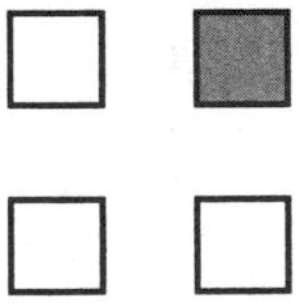		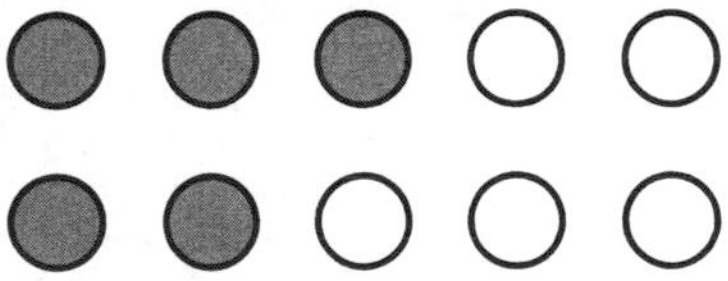
4.	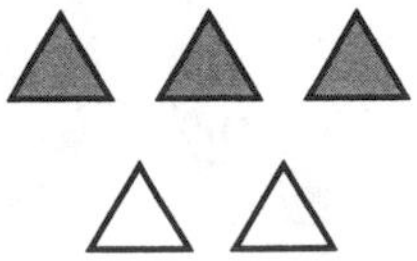	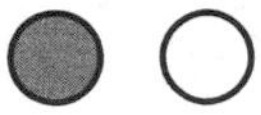	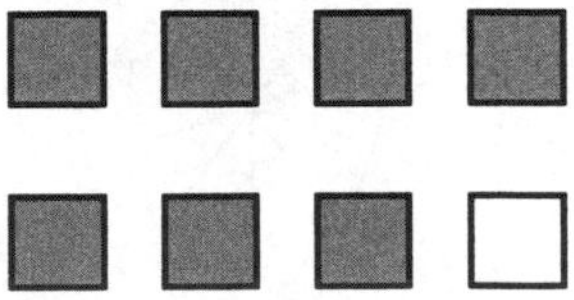

CHAPTER 7 POSTTEST

NAME ______________________

Check What You Learned

Fractions

Use >, <, or = to compare the fractions.

5.

a 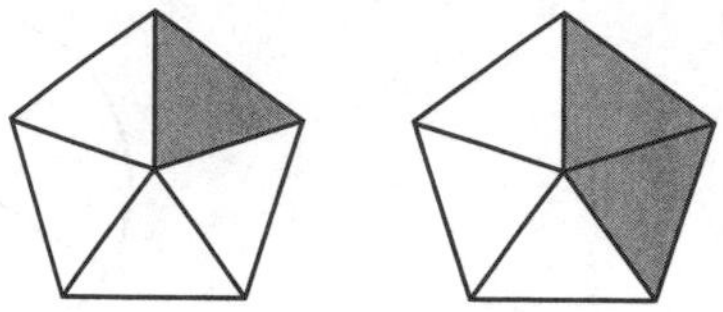

$\frac{1}{5}$ ◯ $\frac{2}{5}$

b 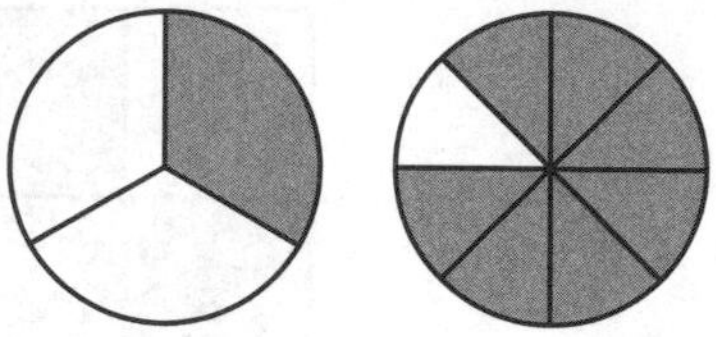

$\frac{1}{3}$ ◯ $\frac{7}{8}$

c 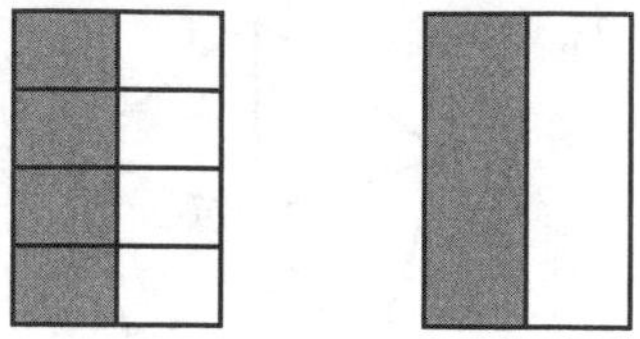

$\frac{4}{8}$ ◯ $\frac{1}{2}$

6.

a 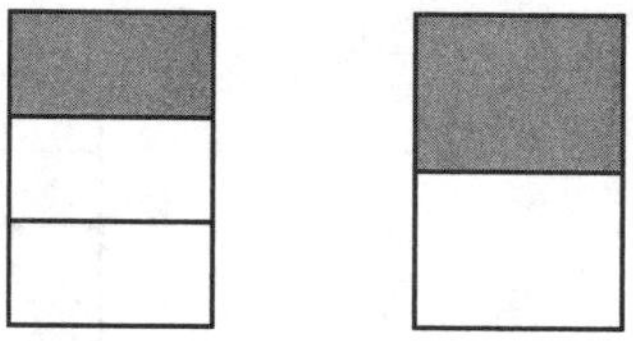

$\frac{1}{3}$ ◯ $\frac{1}{2}$

b 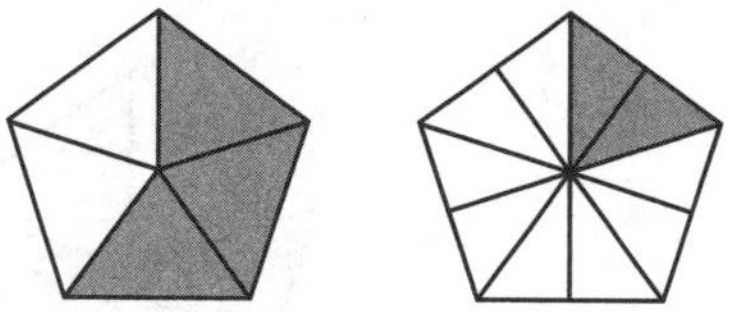

$\frac{3}{5}$ ◯ $\frac{2}{10}$

c 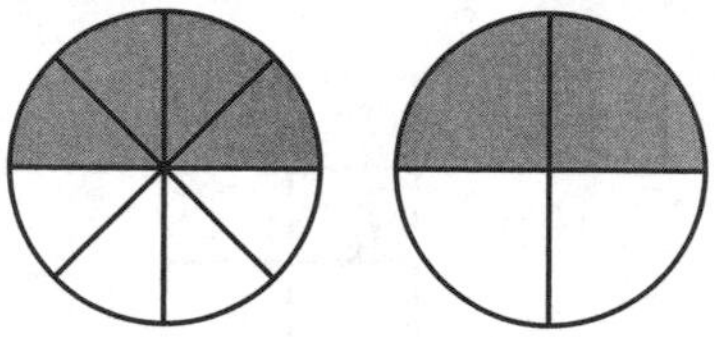

$\frac{4}{8}$ ◯ $\frac{2}{4}$

What fraction of each figure is shaded? Compare the fractions. Use >, <, or =.

7.

a 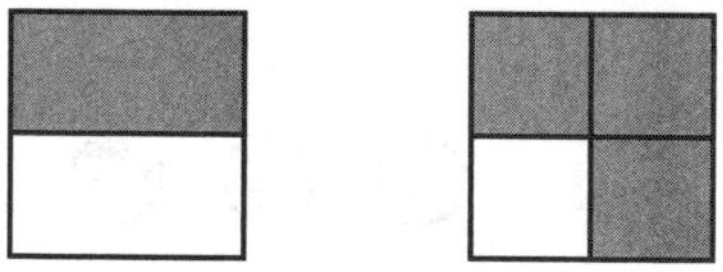

____ ◯ ____

b 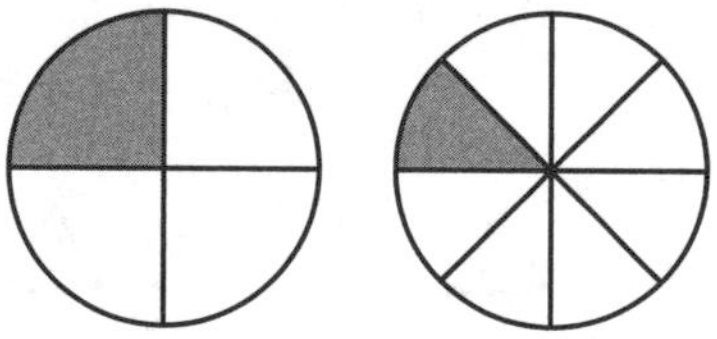

____ ◯ ____

c 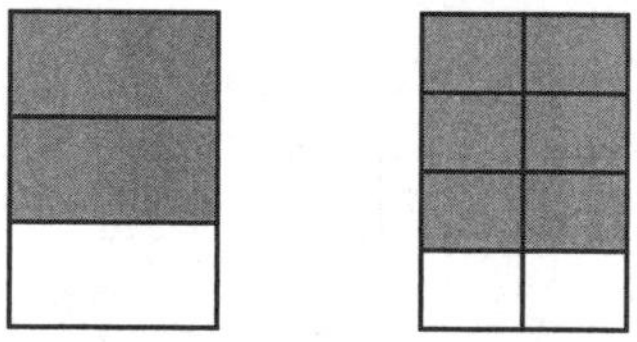

____ ◯ ____

8.

a 

____ ◯ ____

b 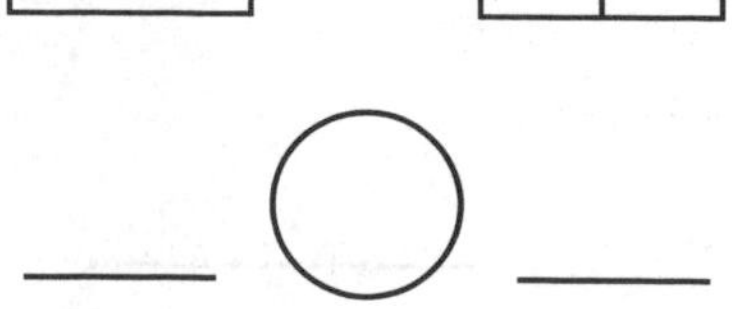

____ ◯ ____

c 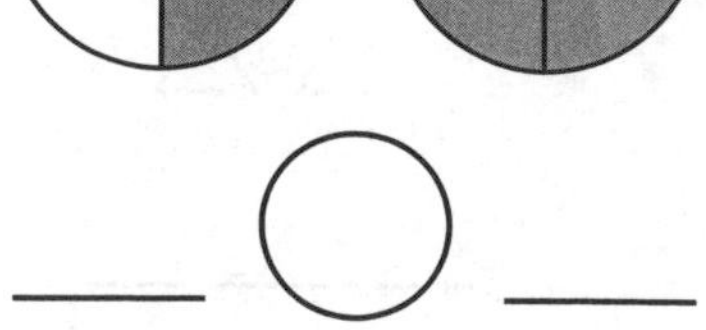

____ ◯ ____

CHAPTER 7 POSTTEST

NAME ___________________

CHAPTER 8 PRETEST

Check What You Know

Customary Measurement

Use a ruler to find the length of each object to the nearest inch.

1. __________ in.

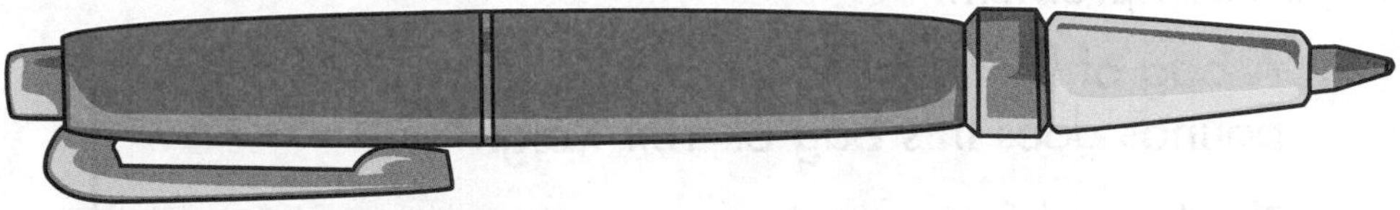

2. __________ in.

3. __________ in.

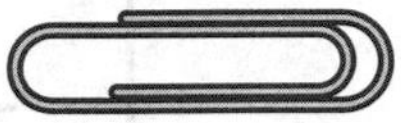

SHOW YOUR WORK

Solve each problem.

4. The rope is 27 feet long. How long is the rope in yards?

The rope is __________ yards long.

5. The book is 12 inches wide. What is the width of the book in feet?

The book is __________ foot wide.

6. At an amusement park, Andrea needs to be 48 inches tall to ride the roller coaster. Andrea is 4 feet tall. Can she ride the roller coaster?

Andrea __________ ride the roller coaster.

7. A cookie recipe calls for 8 ounces of butter. Ryan has 1 pound of butter. Does he have enough butter to make cookies?

Ryan __________ enough butter to make cookies.

8. Sue has 3 gallons of orange juice. How many cups of orange juice does she have?

Sue has __________ cups of orange juice.

4.

5.

6.

7. **8.**

NAME ____________________

Check What You Know

SHOW YOUR WORK

Customary Measurement

Solve each problem.

9. A bag of fruit weighs 32 ounces. How many pounds does this bag of fruit weigh?

The bag of fruit weighs __________ pounds.

10. Which weighs more, 20 ounces or 1 pound?

__________ weighs more.

11. Would you measure a feather in ounces or in pounds?

You would measure a feather in __________.

12. Would you measure the length of a jump rope in inches or feet?

You would measure a jump rope in __________.

13. Would you measure the gasoline in a truck in cups, pints, quarts, or gallons?

You would measure the gasoline in a truck in __________.

14. Would you measure juice in a pitcher by cups or quarts?

You would measure the juice in a pitcher in __________.

15. Four quarts is equal to how many pints?

Four quarts is equal to __________ pints.

16. The thermometer read 93° Fahrenheit at noon. At 5:00 p.m. the thermometer read 80° Fahrenheit. From noon until 5:00 p.m., how much did the temperature decrease?

The temperature decreased __________ °F.

9.	10.
11.	12.
13.	14.
15.	16.

NAME ________________

Lesson 8.1 Measuring in Inches

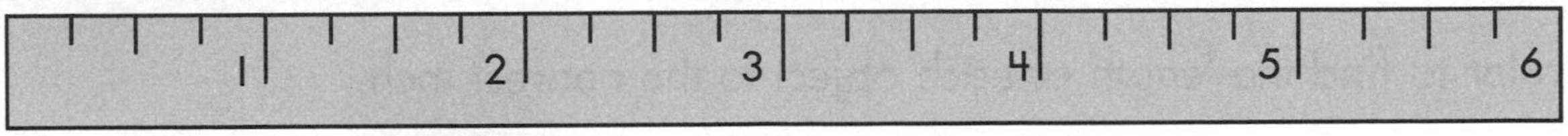

←The toy car is 3 inches (in.) long→

← The piece of string is 5 in. long →

Use a ruler to find the length of each object to the nearest inch.

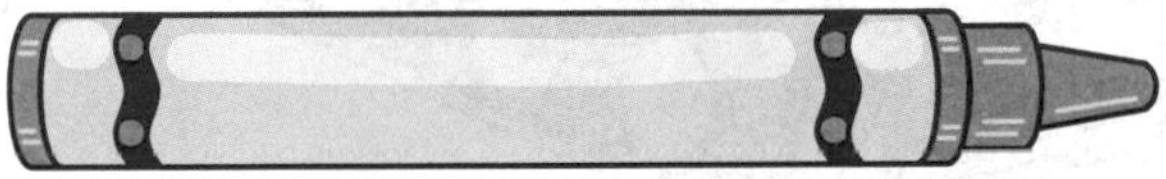

1. __3__ in.

2. __2__ in.

3. __1__ in.

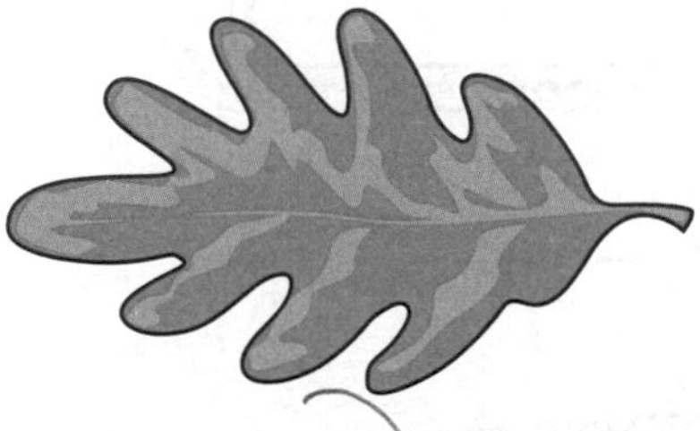

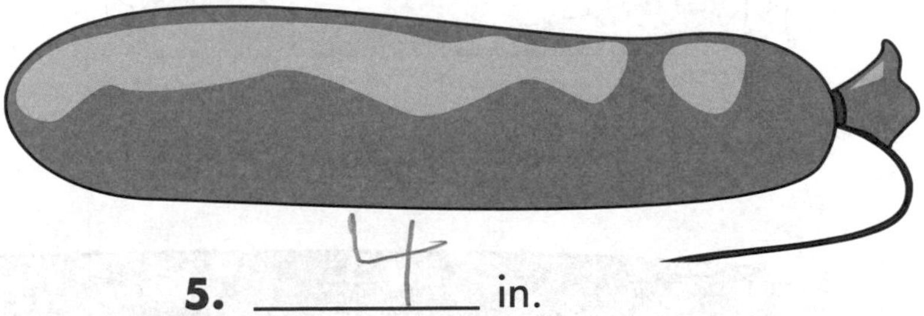

4. __2__ in.

5. __4__ in.

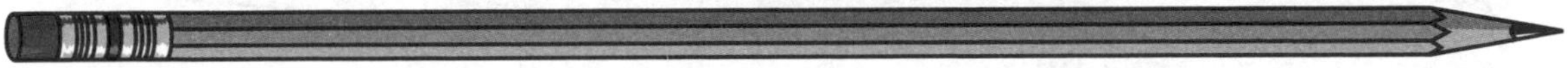

6. __8__ in.

NAME ____________________

Lesson 8.1 Measuring in Inches

Use a ruler to find the length of each object to the nearest inch.

1. ___1___ in.

2. ________ in.

3. ________ in.

4. ________ in.

5. ________ in.

6. ________ in.

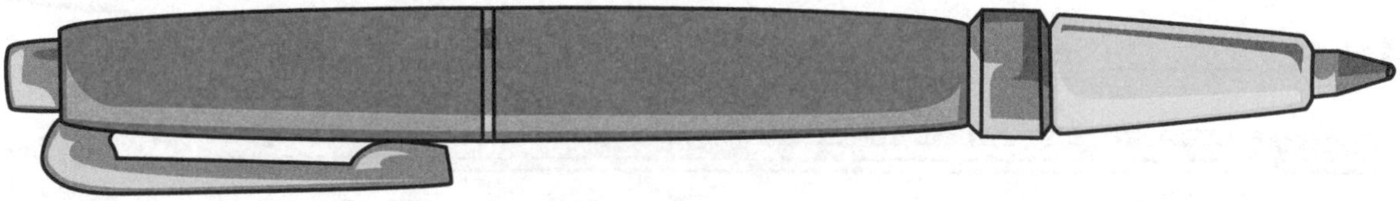

7. ________ in.

NAME ______________________

Lesson 8.2 Converting Units of Length (inches, feet, and yards)

Conversion Table

1 foot (ft.) = 12 inches (in.)

1 yard (yd.) = 3 feet (ft.)

1 yard (yd.) = 36 inches (in.)

When converting from long to short, multiply.

2 ft. = ____ in.
Know: 1 ft. = 12 in.
$2 \times 12 = 24$
2 ft. = 24 in.

When converting from short to long, divide.

9 ft. = ____ yd.
Know: 3 ft. = 1 yd.
$9 \div 3 = 3$
9 ft. = 3 yd.

Complete the following.

	a	b	c
1.	3 ft. = 36 in.	24 in. = ______ ft.	4 yd. = ______ in.
2.	12 in. = ______ ft.	21 ft. = ______ yd.	2 yd. = ______ ft.
3.	36 in. = ______ yd.	5 yd. = ______ in.	6 yd. = ______ in.
4.	5 yd. = ______ ft.	36 in. = ______ ft.	4 yd. = ______ ft.
5.	1 ft. = ______ in.	3 yd. = ______ ft.	6 ft. = ______ yd.
6.	15 ft. = ______ yd.	9 yd. = ______ in.	3 yd. = ______ in.
7.	6 ft. = ______ yd.	27 ft. = ______ yd.	2 ft. = ______ in.
8.	6 ft. = ______ in.	5 ft. = ______ in.	8 yd. = ______ in.
9.	2 yd. = ______ in.	18 ft. = ______ yd.	9 ft. = ______ yd.
10.	12 ft. = ______ yd.	4 ft. = ______ in.	24 ft. = ______ yd.
11.	7 ft. = ______ in.	7 yd. = ______ in.	6 yd. = ______ ft.
12.	3 ft. = ______ yd.	7 yd. = ______ ft.	8 yd. = ______ ft.

NAME ____________________

Lesson 8.3 Measuring Liquid Volume (cups, pints, quarts, and gallons)

Conversion Table
1 pint (pt.) = 2 cups (c.)
1 quart (qt.) = 2 pints (pt.)
1 quart (qt.) = 4 cups (c.)
1 gallon (gal.) = 4 quarts (qt.)
1 gallon (gal.) = 8 pints (pt.)
1 gallon (gal.) = 16 cups (c.)

When converting from more to less, multiply.

7 qt. = ____ pt.
Know: 1 qt. = 2 pt.
$7 \times 2 = 14$
7 qt. = 14 pt.

When converting from less to more, divide.

16 qt. = ____ gal.
Know: 4 qt. = 1 gal.
$16 \div 4 = 4$
16 qt. = 4 gal.

Complete the following.

	a	b	c
1.	2 pt. = 4 c.	32 c. = ______ gal.	40 pt. = ______ gal.
2.	12 c. = ______ qt.	2 gal. = ______ qt.	32 c. = ______ qt.
3.	8 c. = ______ qt.	10 pt. = ______ c.	64 pt. = ______ gal.
4.	4 qt. = ______ c.	3 qt. = ______ pt.	2 c. = ______ pt.
5.	16 c. = ______ gal.	10 pt. = ______ qt.	8 c. = ______ pt.
6.	2 gal. = ______ pt.	16 c. = ______ qt.	5 qt. = ______ c.
7.	5 gal. = ______ qt.	24 qt. = ______ gal.	6 pt. = ______ c.
8.	20 qt. = ______ gal.	14 pt. = ______ qt.	3 gal. = ______ qt.
9.	17 qt. = ______ pt.	32 pt. = ______ gal.	9 gal. = ______ c.
10.	5 gal. = ______ c.	10 c. = ______ pt.	8 qt. = ______ pt.
11.	3 gal. = ______ qt.	16 c. = ______ pt.	10 qt. = ______ c.
12.	16 pt. = ______ gal.	8 pt. = ______ qt.	13 pt. = ______ c.

NAME ______________________

Lesson 8.4 Measuring Weight (ounces and pounds)

Pounds and ounces measure weight.

1 pound (lb.) = 16 ounces (oz.)

A pencil weighs about an ounce.

A can of peas weighs about a pound.

Use the example above to answer questions 1–6.

1. Which weighs more, an ounce or a pound? ________

2. Which weighs less, 18 ounces or 1 pound? ________

3. Which weighs more, 32 ounces of sugar or 2 pounds of sugar? ____________

4. Which weighs less, 14 ounces of cheese or 2 pounds of cheese? ____________

5. Would a toy car be more likely to weigh 5 ounces or 5 pounds? ________

6. Would a television be more likely to weigh 40 ounces or 40 pounds? ________

Tell whether you would use ounces or pounds to measure each of the following.

	a	b	c
7.	a feather ______	a plastic hanger ______	a pumpkin ______
8.	a pack of gum ______	a flower ______	an apricot ______
9.	a table ______	a bag of potting soil ______	a grasshopper ______
10.	a bucket of rocks ______	a baby ______	a turkey ______

NAME ______________________

Lesson 8.5 Temperature

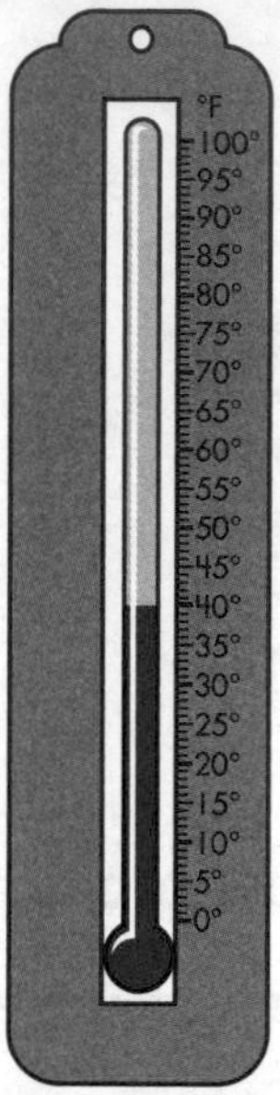

A thermometer measures the temperature in degrees Fahrenheit.

Water will freeze at 32 degrees Fahrenheit (32°F).

The temperature on this thermometer is 40 degrees Fahrenheit (40°F).

What is the temperature reading on each thermometer?

1.

a

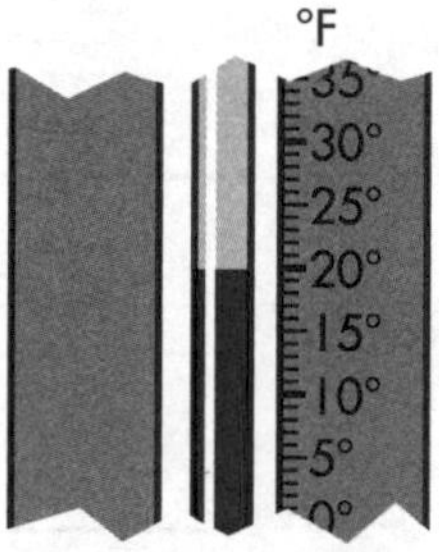

20 °F

b

____ °F

c

____ °F

2.

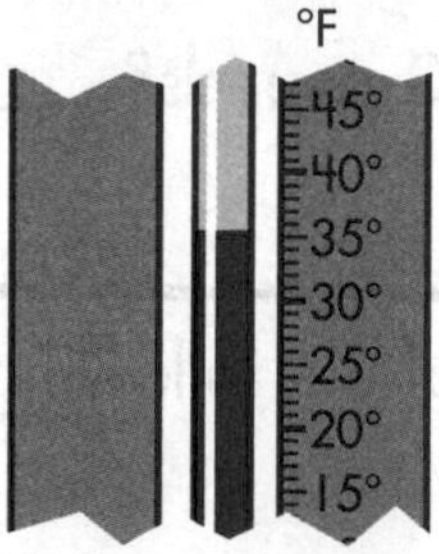

____ °F

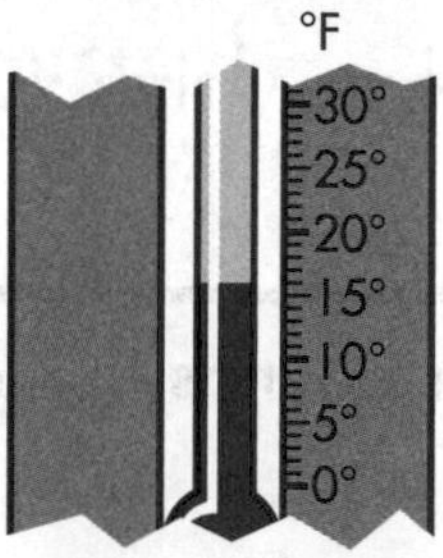

____ °F

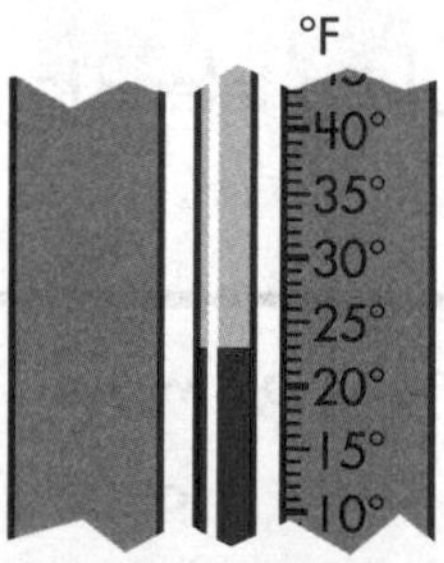

____ °F

3.

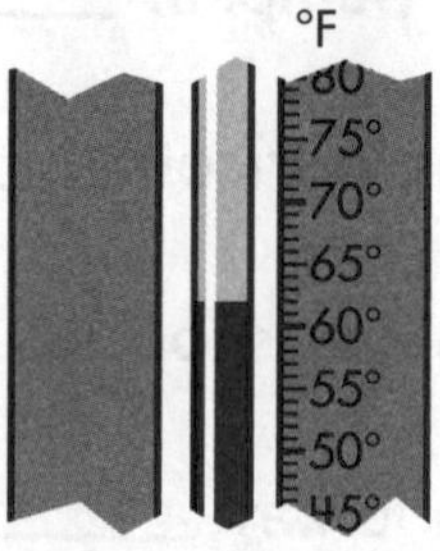

____ °F

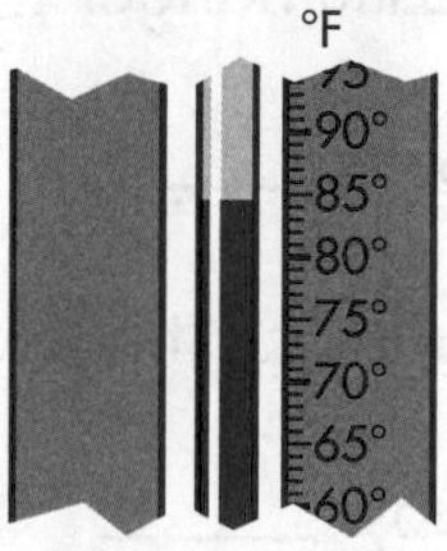

____ °F

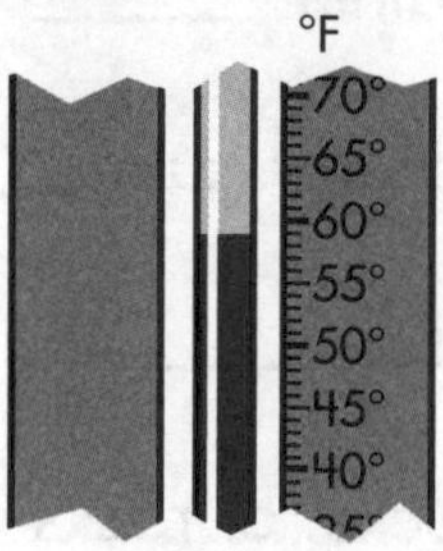

____ °F

NAME ____________________

Lesson 8.6 Problem Solving

SHOW YOUR WORK

Solve each problem.

1. Danny caught a fish that was 2 feet long. How long was the fish in inches?

The fish was ________ inches long.

2. Ashley is 48 inches tall. How tall is she in feet?

Ashley is ________ feet tall.

3. A recipe calls for 4 cups of water. How many pints of water is the recipe calling for?

The recipe is calling for ________ pints of water.

4. Jim had 2 gallons of paint. He used 6 quarts. How many quarts does he have left?

Jim has ________ quarts left.

5. Would you measure the water in a swimming pool in cups, pints, quarts, or gallons?

You would measure the water in a swimming pool in ________.

6. Would you measure the juice in a glass in cups, pints, quarts, or gallons?

You would measure the juice in ________.

7. The thermometer reads 34° Fahrenheit. Is this measurement considered hot or cold?

This measurement is considered ________.

8. The thermometer reads 89° Fahrenheit. Is this measurement considered hot or cold?

This measurement is considered ________.

1.	**2.**
3.	**4.**
5.	**6.**
7.	**8.**

NAME ____________________

Lesson 8.7 Problem Solving

SHOW YOUR WORK

Solve each problem.

1. Hiroshi is 3 feet 10 inches tall. His brother, Akira, is 48 inches tall. Who is taller?

Hiroshi is __________ inches tall.

Akira is __________ inches tall.

__________ is taller.

2. A table is 2 yards in length. How long is it in feet?

The table is __________ feet long.

3. Would you measure a toy car in inches, feet, or yards?

You would measure a toy car in __________.

4. Would you measure the length of a football field in inches, feet, or yards?

You would measure a football field in __________.

5. Inez weighed 6 pounds at birth. How many ounces did she weigh at birth?

Inez weighed __________ ounces at birth.

6. Would you measure a dog in ounces or pounds?

You would measure a dog in __________.

7. The thermometer read 63° Fahrenheit. How many degrees is this above the temperature at which water freezes?

The thermometer reads __________°F.

Water freezes at __________°F.

It is __________°F above freezing.

1.	
2.	**3.**
4.	**5.**
6.	**7.**

NAME ________________________

Check What You Learned

Customary Measurement

Use a ruler to find the length of each object to the nearest inch.

1. ________ in.

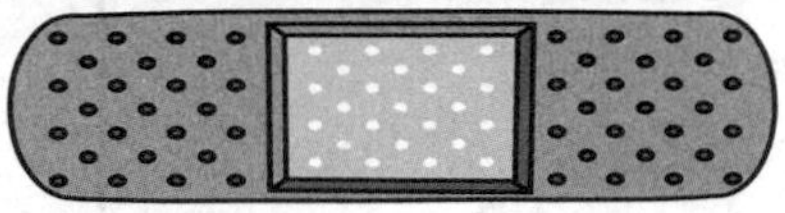

2. ________ in.

3. ________ in.

CHAPTER 8 POSTTEST

SHOW YOUR WORK

Solve each problem.

4. Ruth needs 5 yards of fabric. How many feet of fabric does Ruth need?

   Ruth needs _____ feet of fabric.

5. A truck has a height of 8 feet 11 inches. It needs to go under a bridge that has a clearance of 96 inches. Can the truck go under this bridge?

   The truck ________ go under this bridge.

6. At the age of 5, Tom was 3 feet 4 inches tall. When he was 8 years old he was 4 feet tall. How many inches did Tom grow?

   Tom grew _____ inches.

7. A recipe calls for 5 quarts of water. How many cups of water does it call for?

   The recipe calls for _____ cups of water.

8. Mr. Armas drank 16 cups of coffee in one week. How many gallons of coffee did Mr. Armas drink in 1 week?

   Mr. Armas drank _____ gallon(s) of coffee in 1 week.

4.	
5.	
6.	
7.	8.

NAME ____________________

Check What You Learned

SHOW YOUR WORK

Customary Measurement

Solve each problem.

9. Which weighs more, a 30-ounce bag of fruit or a 3-pound bag of vegetables?

The __________ weigh(s) more.

10. Lucy wants to buy 5 quarts of cream. At the grocery store, cream only comes in pint containers. How many pint containers will Lucy need to buy to equal 5 quarts of cream?

Lucy will need to buy _____ pint containers to equal five quarts of cream.

11. Would a chair be more likely to weigh 5 ounces or 5 pounds?

A chair would more likely weigh __________.

12. Would you be more likely to measure the length of a swimming pool in inches or yards?

You would measure a swimming pool in ________.

13. Would you be more likely to measure the height of an adult in inches or feet?

You would measure an adult in __________.

14. Would you measure the amount of water in a glass in cups, pints, or quarts?

You would measure the water in a glass in _____.

15. Today, the thermometer reads 86° Fahrenheit. How many degrees is that above the point at which water freezes?

It is _____ °F above freezing.

9.	**10.**
11.	**12.**
13.	**14.**
15.	

CHAPTER 8 POSTTEST

Check What You Know

Metric Measurement

Use a ruler to find the length of each object to the nearest centimeter.

1. ________ cm 

2. ________ cm 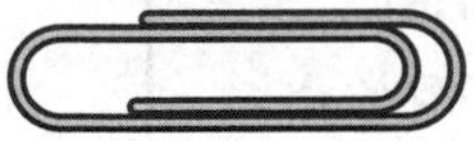

3. ________ cm 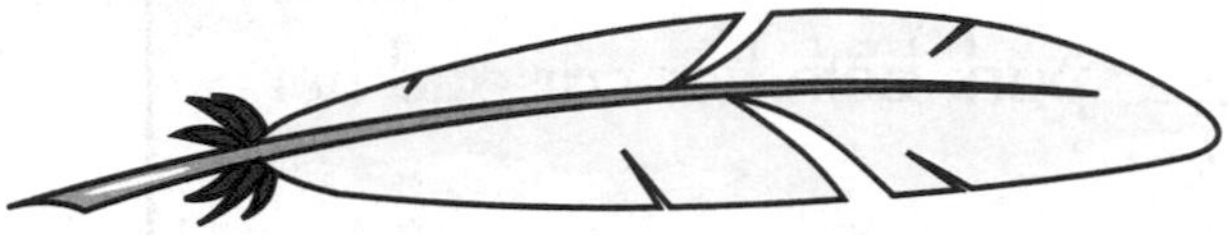

Complete the following.

	a	b	c
4.	2 m = _____ cm	5,000 g = _____ kg	8,000 mL = _____ L
5.	5,000 mg = _____ g	1 L = _____ mL	5 m = _____ cm
6.	5 L = _____ mL	7 kg = _____ g	7 g = _____ mg
7.	300 cm = _____ m	3 m = _____ cm	4,000 mL = _____ L
8.	5 kg = _____ g	2 g = _____ mg	200 cm = _____ m
9.	4 m = _____ cm	6,000 mg = _____ g	6 m = _____ cm

What is the temperature reading on each thermometer?

10.

a

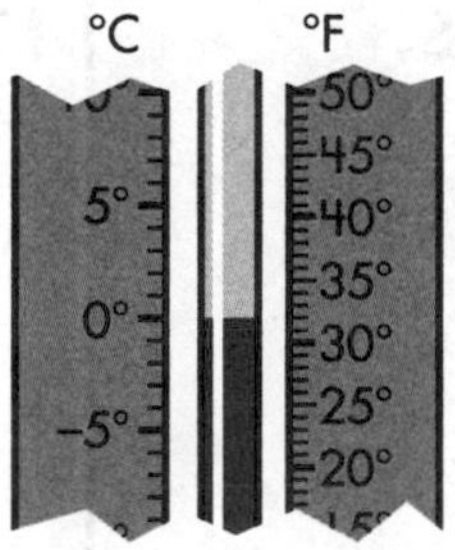

_____ °C _____ °F

b

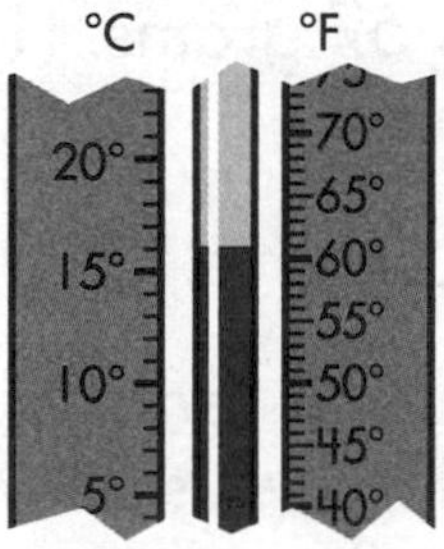

_____ °C _____ °F

c

_____ °C _____ °F

NAME ____________________

CHAPTER 9 PRETEST

Check What You Know

Metric Measurement

SHOW YOUR WORK

Solve each problem.

11. Mrs. Chen's driveway is 6 meters long. Her car is 2 meters 23 centimeters long. Her truck is 3 meters 95 centimeters long. Can Mrs. Chen park both her car and her truck in her driveway?

Mrs. Chen ________ park both her car and her truck in her driveway.

12. Tina is 1 meter 44 centimeters tall. Shawn is 124 centimeters tall. Who is taller?

________ is taller.

13. A carton contains 2 liters of juice. If 1,300 milliliters are used, how many milliliters are left?

There are ________ milliliters of juice left.

14. A 1-liter container has 5 servings in it. How many milliliters is each serving?

Each serving is ________ milliliters.

15. The saltshaker holds 5 grams of salt. If a grain of salt weighs 1 milligram, how many grains of salt are in the saltshaker?

There are ________ grains of salt in the saltshaker.

16. A plant weighs 6 kilograms 57 grams. How much does the plant weigh in grams?

The plant weighs ________ grams.

17. In the morning, the thermometer read 46° Celsius. In the afternoon, it read 34° Celsius. How much did the temperature decrease?

The temperature decreased ________°C.

11.	
12.	**13.**
14.	**15.**
16.	**17.**

NAME ______________________________

Lesson 9.1 Measuring in Centimeters

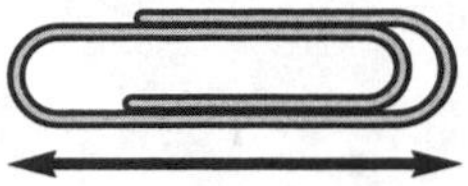

The paper clip is 3 centimeters or 3 cm long.

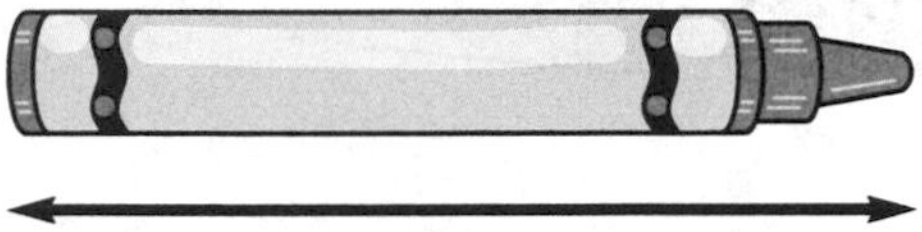

The crayon is 6 cm long.

Use a ruler to find the length of each object to the nearest centimeter.

1. 14 cm

2. ______ cm

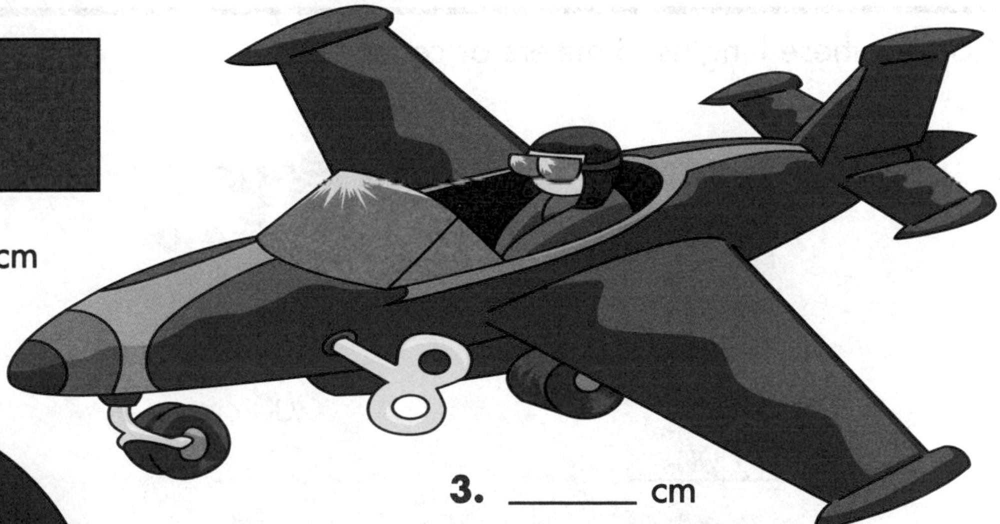

3. ______ cm

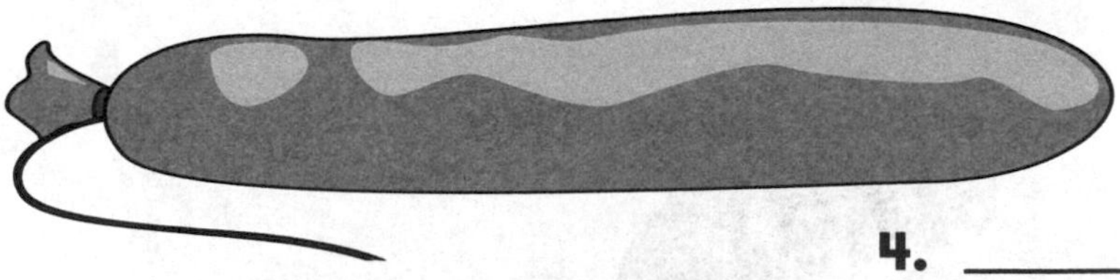

4. ______ cm

5. ______ cm

6. ______ cm

NAME ____________________

Lesson 9.1 Measuring in Centimeters

Use a ruler to find the length of each object to the nearest centimeter.

1. ____6____ cm 

2. __________ cm 

3. __________ cm 

1 meter (m) = 100 centimeters (cm)

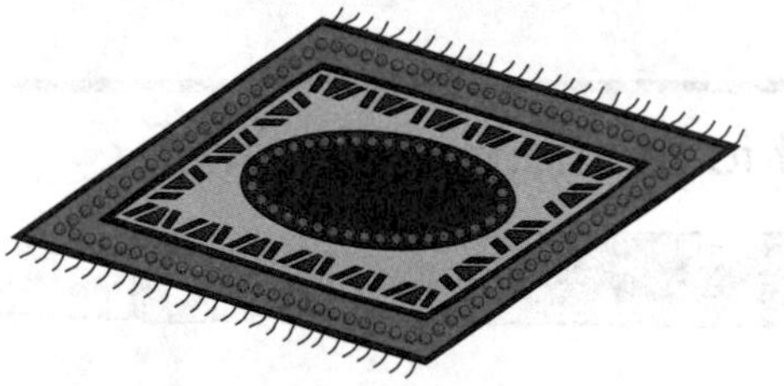

This rug is 200 cm long.

How long is it in meters?

The rug is 2 m long.

Convert these lengths to meters or centimeters.

	a	b	c

4.	10 m	200 cm	600 cm
	___1,000___ cm	______ m	______ m

5.	12 m	3 m	2 m
	______ cm	______ cm	______ cm

NAME ________________________

Lesson 9.2 Measuring Liquid Volume (liters)

A liter (L) is used to measure liquid volume.

A single serving of fruit juice is usually sold by the liter.

1 liter (L) = 1,000 milliliters (mL)

Complete the following.

	a	b	c
1.	3 L = 3,000 mL	2 L = ________ mL	7,000 mL = ________ L
2.	2,000 mL = ________ L	4,000 mL = ________ L	5 L = ________ mL

Answer the following questions.

3. Which is less, 500 milliliters or 5 liters? ________

4. Which is more, 4,534 milliliters or 4 liters? ________

5. Would the water in a wading pool be more likely to be 500 liters or 500 milliliters? ________

6. Would a glass of juice be more likely to be 300 milliliters or 300 liters? ________

Write whether you would use milliliters or liters to measure each of the following.

	a	b	c
7.	a bucket of water liters	a bottle of liquid soap ________	a bottle of perfume ________
8.	a bottle of lotion ________	a watering can full of water ________	a pitcher of lemonade ________

NAME ______________________

Lesson 9.3 Measuring Weight (grams and kilograms)

Conversion Table
1 gram (g) = 1,000 milligrams (mg)
1 kilogram (kg) = 1,000 grams (g)

A grain of sand weighs about 1 mg.

A safety pin weighs about 1 g.

A jar of peanut butter weighs about 1 kg.

Use the information above to answer questions 1–4.

1. Which weighs more, a gram or a milligram? __________

2. Which weighs less, a gram or a kilogram? __________

3. How many safety pins would weigh the same as one jar of peanut butter? __________

4. 3,000 grains of sand would equal how many safety pins? __________

Write whether you would use milligrams (mg), grams (g), or kilograms (kg) to measure each of the following.

	a	b	c
5.	a baby	a grain of salt	a brick
	kilograms	__________	__________
6.	a couch	a raindrop	an ice cube
	__________	__________	__________
7.	a paper clip	a sugar cube	an umbrella
	__________	__________	__________
8.	a feather	a pencil	a shoe
	__________	__________	__________

NAME ____________________

Lesson 9.4 Temperature

A thermometer can measure the temperature in degrees Fahrenheit (°F) and in degrees Celsius (°C).

Water freezes at 0 degrees Celsius (0°C).

Water freezes at 32 degrees Fahrenheit (32°F).

The temperature on this thermometer is 20 degrees Celsius (20°C). It is also at 68°F. 20°C is equivalent to 68°F.

What is the temperature reading on each thermometer? Give the temperature in Celsius and in Fahrenheit. Always measure to the nearest degree.

a

1. 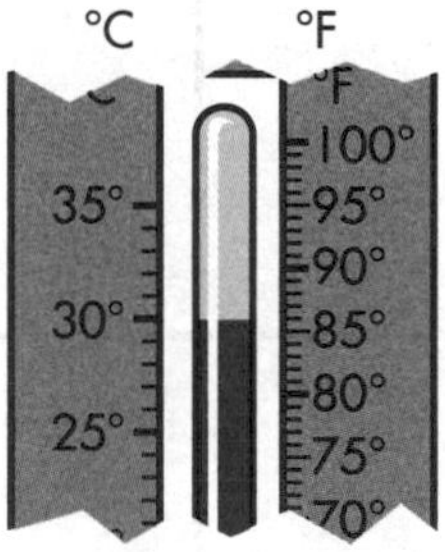

30 °C

86 °F

b

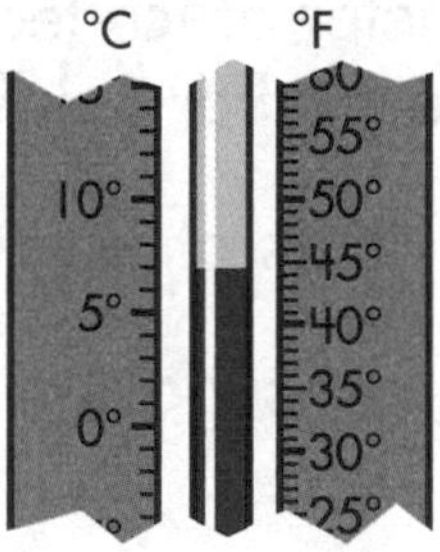

____ °C

____ °F

c

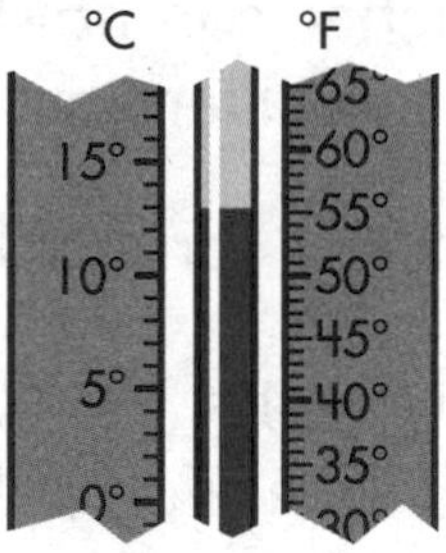

____ °C

____ °F

2. 

____ °C

____ °F

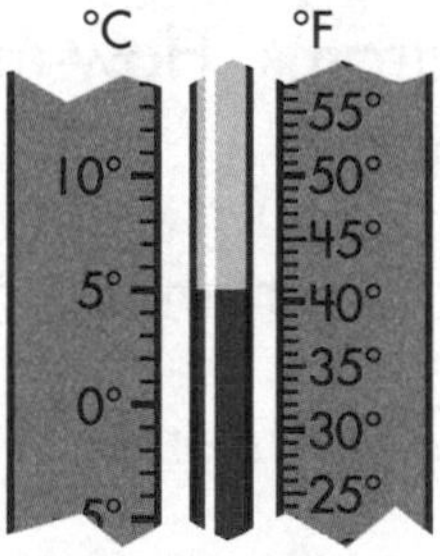

____ °C

____ °F

____ °C

____ °F

3. 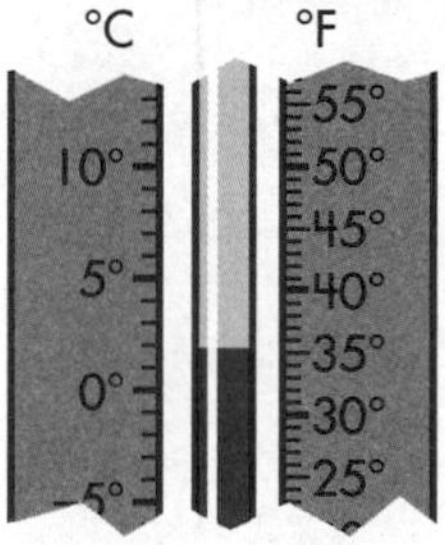

____ °C

____ °F

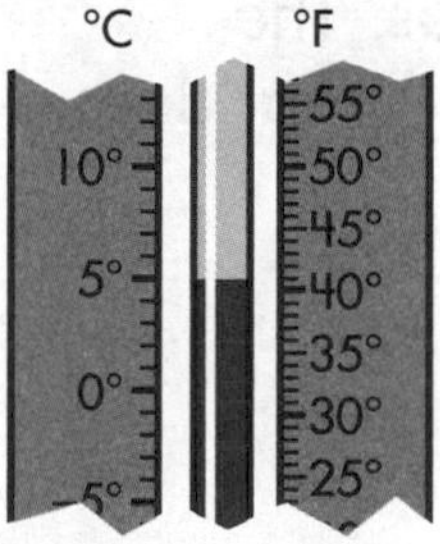

____ °C

____ °F

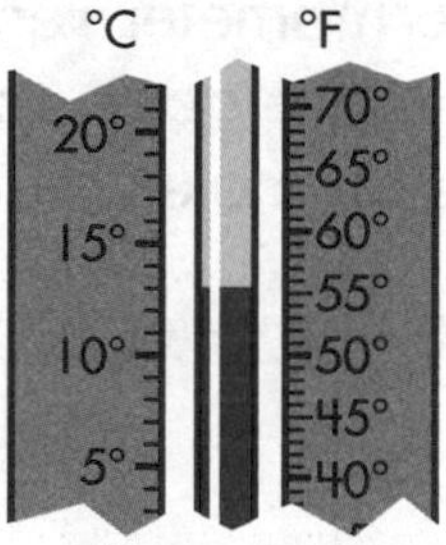

____ °C

____ °F

NAME ____________________

Lesson 9.5 Problem Solving

SHOW YOUR WORK

Solve each problem.

1. A pencil is 10 centimeters long. How many pencils laid end–to–end would it take to equal 1 meter?

It would take __________ pencils.

2. A couch measured 2 meters in length. How many centimeters in length is it?

It is __________ centimeter in length.

3. Would you use liters or milliliters to measure a glass of tomato juice?

You would use __________.

4. The pitcher can hold 3,000 millimeter of ice tea. How many liters of ice tea can the pitcher hold?

The pitcher can hold __________ liters of ice tea.

5. Which weighs more, 1,000 grams of sugar or 2 kilograms of sugar?

The __________ of sugar weighs more.

6. A sugar cube weighs 2,000 milligrams. How much does the sugar cube weigh in grams?

The sugar cube weighs __________ grams.

7. Which is hotter, 10° Celsius or 10° Fahrenheit?

__________ is hotter.

8. The thermometer reads 13° Celsius. The temperature goes up 10° Celsius. What does the thermometer read now?

The thermometer reads__________°C now.

1.	**2.**
3.	**4.**
5.	**6.**
7.	**8.**

NAME ____________________

Check What You Learned

Metric Measurement

Use a ruler to find the length of each object to the nearest centimeter.

2. __________ cm

1. __________ cm

3. __________ cm

Complete the following.

	a	b	c
4.	300 cm = _____ m	5,000 mg = _____ g	400 cm = _____ m
5.	200 cm = _____ m	5 m = _____ cm	6 m = _____ cm
6.	3 g = _____ mg	8,000 g = _____ kg	5,000 mL = _____ L
7.	6,000 mL = _____ L	3,000 g = _____ kg	7 m = _____ cm
8.	7,000 mg = _____ g	4,000 mL = _____ L	2,000 mL = _____ L
9.	5 L = _____ mL	7 g = _____ mg	8 kg = _____ g

What is the temperature reading on each thermometer?

10.

a

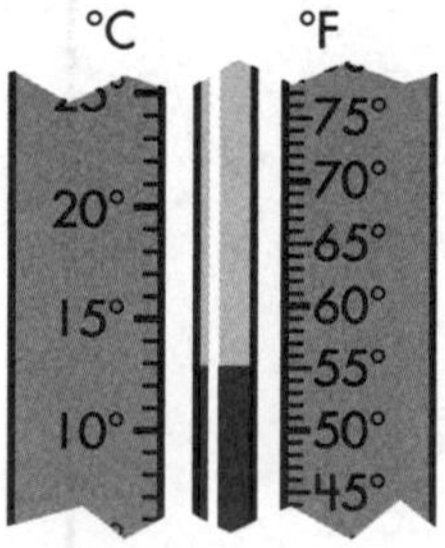

_____ °C _____ °F

b

_____ °C _____ °F

c

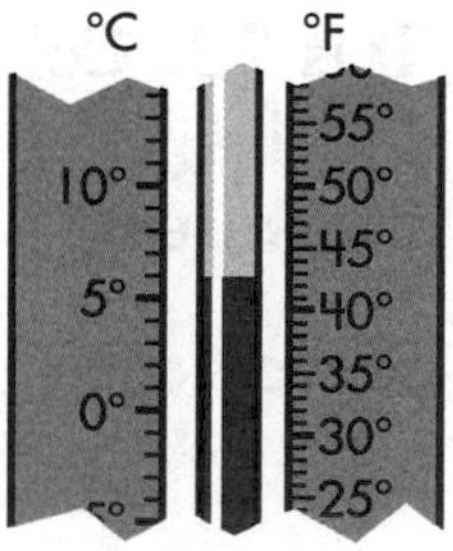

_____ °C _____ °F

NAME ____________________

Check What You Learned

SHOW YOUR WORK

Metric Measurement

Solve each problem.

11. Suni is 1 meter 3 centimeters tall. How tall is Suni in centimeters?

Suni is __________ centimeters tall.

12. Mr. Thomas's garden is 2 meters 15 centimeters long. It is 1 meter 23 centimeters wide. How long and wide is his garden in centimeters?

The garden is __________ centimeters long and __________ centimeters wide.

13. Christopher has 1 liter of milk. He uses 300 milliliters of the milk in a recipe. How many milliliters of milk does he have left?

Christopher has __________ milliliters of milk left.

14. A teakettle can hold 2 liters of water. How many milliliters does the teakettle hold?

The teakettle holds __________ milliliters of water.

15. Alice weighs 95 kilograms. How many grams does she weigh?

Alice weighs __________ grams.

16. It is 23° Celsius in the morning. By noon, it is 46° Celsius. How many degrees did the temperature increase?

It increased __________°C.

11.	**12.**
13.	**14.**
15.	**16.**

CHAPTER 9 POSTTEST

NAME ____________________

Check What You Know

Money, Time, and Calendar

Complete the following.

1. 30 pennies have a value of ________ cents or ________ nickels.

2. 50 pennies have a value of ________ cents or ________ half dollar.

3. $3.23 means ________ dollars and ________ cents.

4. $10.09 means ________ dollars and ________ cents.

Add or subtract.

	a	b	c	d	e
5.	$ 3.06 .45 + 13.92	$23.57 − 16.43	62¢ +19¢	96¢ −43¢	$ 6.45 13.96 + 22.42

Write the value of each collection.

6.

a

____

b

____

Compare the two sets of collections. Use "greater than," "less than," or "equal to."

7.

____

____

________ is ________ ________.

NAME ____________________

Check What You Know

Money, Time, and Calendar

Determine the change for the following.

8. A yoyo costs $3.53.

money value $ ______

cost of yoyo − ______

change $ ______

Complete the following.

	a	b
9.	2:32 means ___ minutes after ___.	2:32 means ___ minutes to ___.
10.	3:45 means ___ minutes after ___.	3:45 means ___ minutes to ___.
11.	7:06 means ___ minutes after ___.	9:50 means ___ minutes to ___.

Tell the time to the nearest hour, half hour, quarter hour, or minute as indicated.

12.

a	b	c	d
hour	half hour	quarter hour	minute
___ : ___	___ : ___	___ : ___	___ : ___

Complete the following.

	a	b	c
13.	There are _____ days in a year.	There are _____ months in a year.	There are _____ days in a week.
14.	There are _____ hours in a day.	There are _____ minutes in an hour.	February _____ occurs only in leap years.
15.	2 hours 3 minutes _____ minutes	63 minutes _____ hour 3 minutes	1 day 2 hours _____ hours

NAME ____________________

Lesson 10.1 Money: Using Decimals

1 penny	1 nickel	1 dime	1 quarter	1 half dollar	1 dollar
1 cent	5 cents	10 cents	25 cents	50 cents	100 cents
1¢	5¢	10¢	25¢	50¢	100¢
or	or	or	or	or	or
$0.01	$0.05	$0.10	$0.25	$0.50	$1.00

10 pennies have a value of __10__ cents or __1__ dime.

15 pennies have a value of __15__ cents or __3__ nickels.

$5.52 means __5__ dollars and __52__ cents.

$7.03 means __7__ dollars and __3__ cents.

Complete the following.

1. 20 pennies have a value of _____ cents or _____ dimes.

2. 50 pennies have a value of _____ cents or _____ quarters.

3. 2 quarters have a value of _____ cents or _____ half dollar.

4. 10 dimes have a value of _____ cents or _____ dollar.

5. 5 nickels have a value of _____ cents or _____ quarter.

6. 30 pennies have a value of _____ cents or _____ dimes.

7. $17.43 means _____ dollars and _____ cents.

8. $16.07 means _____ dollars and _____ cents.

9. $5.95 means _____ dollars and _____ cents.

10. $3.23 means _____ dollars and _____ cents.

11. $12.50 means _____ dollars and _____ cents.

12. $9.17 means _____ dollars and _____ cents.

NAME ____________________

Lesson 10.2 Money: Adding and Subtracting with Decimals

Be sure to line up the decimal points.

Add or subtract as usual.

Put a decimal point (.) and a $ or ¢ in the answer.

$10.03 + .96 $10.99	45¢ +22¢ 67¢	$9.87 − 6.52 $3.35	76¢ −29¢ 47¢

Add or subtract.

	a	b	c	d	e
1.	$2.03 + 5.97 $8.00	$13.56 + 1.72	$56.96 + 5.42	$7.52 + 3.85	$40.30 + .47
2.	$ 3.59 22.19 + 6.70	$4.36 3.52 + .46	$22.59 13.21 + 5.50	46¢ 13¢ +30¢	$13.57 20.92 + 4.16
3.	$25.36 − 1.24	$56.43 − 33.29	$96.00 − 17.00	$9.20 − .86	54¢ −23¢
4.	73¢ −69¢	$72.83 − 13.72	$54.00 − 30.00	$19.23 − 8.17	$4.05 − .44
5.	63¢ +19¢	93¢ −56¢	$13.93 + 7.21	$24.36 − 13.93	$45.23 − 19.00
6.	$5.43 − .92	$7.92 + 1.09	54¢ +29¢	93¢ −58¢	$59.92 − 7.80

Lesson 10.3 Counting Money

$5.00

$1.00

50¢ or $0.50

25¢ or $0.25

10¢ or $0.10

5¢ or $0.05

1¢ or $0.01

$$\begin{array}{r} \$2.00 \\ .50 \\ +\ .03 \\ \hline \$2.53 \end{array}$$

2 dollars and 53 cents is $2.53.

Write the value of each collection.

a **b**

1. 
82¢

____

2. 
____

____

3. 
____

____

NAME ____________________

Lesson 10.3 Counting Money

58¢

63¢

58¢ is less than 63¢.

Compare the two sets of collections. Use "greater than," "less than," or "equal to."

1.  50¢ |  50¢

50¢ is equal to 50¢.

2.  ______ |  ______

______ is ______ ______.

3.  ______ |  ______

______ is ______ ______.

4.  ______ |  ______

______ is ______ ______.

NAME ____________________

Lesson 10.4 Making Change

A candy bar costs 79¢.

money value	$ 1.3 2
cost of candy bar	– .7 9
change	$ 0.5 3

Determine the change for the following.

1. A book costs $4.34.

money value	$ 6.50
cost of book	– 4.34
change	$ 2.16

2. A calculator costs $6.82.

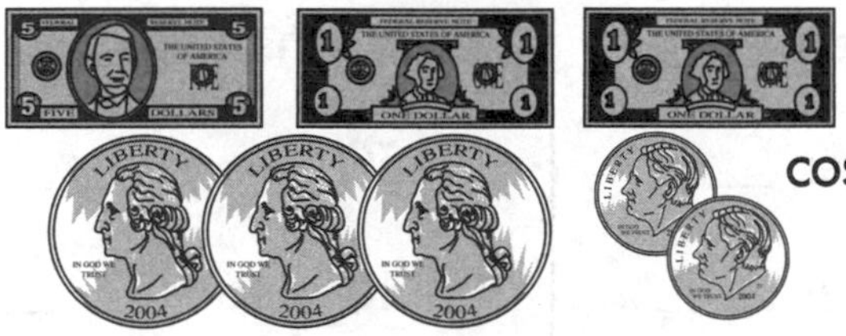

money value	$ ______
cost of calculator	– ______
change	$ ______

3. A pack of gum costs $1.23.

money value	$ ______
cost of gum	– ______
change	$ ______

4. A dictionary costs $3.46.

money value	$ ______
cost of dictionary	– ______
change	$ ______

5. A roll of film costs $2.57.

money value	$ ______
cost of film	– ______
change	$ ______

NAME ________________________

Lesson 10.5 Telling Time

5:15 is read "five fifteen" and means "15 minutes after 5."

12:50 is read "twelve fifty" and means "50 minutes after 12" or "10 minutes to 1."

4:45 is read "four forty-five" and means "45 minutes after 5" or "15 minutes to 6."

Complete the following.

	a	b
1.	6:15 means __15__ minutes after __6__.	11:50 means ____ minutes to ____.
2.	7:50 means ____ minutes after ____.	7:50 means ____ minutes to ____.
3.	12:45 means ____ minutes after ____.	12:45 means ____ minutes to ____.
4.	1:30 means ____ minutes after ____.	1:30 means ____ minutes to ____.

For each analog clock face, write the numerals that name the time.

a **b** **c** **d**

5.

___ : ___

___ : ___

___ : ___

___ : ___

6.

___ : ___

___ : ___

___ : ___

___ : ___

NAME ____________________

Lesson 10.5 Telling Time

6:41

The closest hour on an analog clock is determined by the hour hand (the short hand).

The closest half hour, quarter hour, and minute are determined by the minute hand (the long hand).

A half hour is at 30 minutes or 1 hour.

A quarter hour is at 15, 30, 45 minutes, or 1 hour.

What time is it to the nearest hour? 7:00, half hour? 6:30, quarter hour? 6:45, minute? 6:41

Write the time to the nearest hour, half hour, quarter hour, or minute as indicated.

		a	b	c	d
1.		hour ___ : ___	half hour ___ : ___	quarter hour ___ : ___	minute ___ : ___
2.		hour ___ : ___	half hour ___ : ___	quarter hour ___ : ___	minute ___ : ___

Draw the hands on the analog clock to express the time presented on the digital clock.

a

3. 

b

4. 

NAME ______________________

Lesson 10.6 Calendar

January

S	M	T	W	T	F	S
			1	2	3	4
5	6	7	8	9	10	11
12	13	14	15	16	17	18
19	20	21	22	23	24	25
26	27	28	29	30	31	

February

S	M	T	W	T	F	S
						1
2	3	4	5	6	7	8
9	10	11	12	13	14	15
16	17	18	19	20	21	22
23	24	25	26	27	28	

March

S	M	T	W	T	F	S
						1
2	3	4	5	6	7	8
9	10	11	12	13	14	15
16	17	18	19	20	21	22
23	24	25	26	27	28	29
30	31					

April

S	M	T	W	T	F	S
		1	2	3	4	5
6	7	8	9	10	11	12
13	14	15	16	17	18	19
20	21	22	23	24	25	26
27	28	29	30			

May

S	M	T	W	T	F	S
				1	2	3
4	5	6	7	8	9	10
11	12	13	14	15	16	17
18	19	20	21	22	23	24
25	26	27	28	29	30	31

June

S	M	T	W	T	F	S
1	2	3	4	5	6	7
8	9	10	11	12	13	14
15	16	17	18	19	20	21
22	23	24	25	26	27	28
29	30					

July

S	M	T	W	T	F	S
		1	2	3	4	5
6	7	8	9	10	11	12
13	14	15	16	17	18	19
20	21	22	23	24	25	26
27	28	29	30	31		

August

S	M	T	W	T	F	S
					1	2
3	4	5	6	7	8	9
10	11	12	13	14	15	16
17	18	19	20	21	22	23
24	25	26	27	28	29	30
31						

September

S	M	T	W	T	F	S
	1	2	3	4	5	6
7	8	9	10	11	12	13
14	15	16	17	18	19	20
21	22	23	24	25	26	27
28	29	30				

October

S	M	T	W	T	F	S
			1	2	3	4
5	6	7	8	9	10	11
12	13	14	15	16	17	18
19	20	21	22	23	24	25
26	27	28	29	30	31	

November

S	M	T	W	T	F	S
						1
2	3	4	5	6	7	8
9	10	11	12	13	14	15
16	17	18	19	20	21	22
23	24	25	26	27	28	29
30						

December

S	M	T	W	T	F	S
	1	2	3	4	5	6
7	8	9	10	11	12	13
14	15	16	17	18	19	20
21	22	23	24	25	26	27
28	29	30	31			

There are $365\frac{1}{4}$ days in a year. A leap year occurs every four years. In a **leap year,** February 29 is added to combine the $\frac{1}{4}$ days into 1 day. In a leap year calendar, there are 366 days. In all other calendar years there are 365 days.

Answer each question. Use the calendar to help you.

	a		b	
1.	How many months are in a year?	_____	How many months have 31 days?	_____
2.	How many days are in December?	_____	How many days are in February?	_____
3.	How many days are in February during a leap year?	_____	How many months have exactly 30 days?	_____
4.	How many days are in a week?	_____	How many full weeks are in May?	_____
5.	On what day is August 2?	_____	How many Mondays are in January?	_____
6.	What date falls 23 days before June 2?	_____	What date falls 16 days after September 29?	_____

There are 60 minutes in an hour. There are 24 hours in a day. Complete the following.

	a	b	c	d
7.	2 hours 15 minutes ___ minutes	1 hour 50 minutes ___ minutes	120 minutes ___ hours	180 minutes ___ hours
8.	1 day 2 hours ___ hours	2 days 5 hours ___ hours	29 hours ___ day(s) ___ hours	48 hours ___ days

NAME ____________________

Check What You Learned

Money, Time, and Calendar

Complete the following.

1. 25 pennies have a value of ________ cents or ________ quarter.

2. 4 quarters have a value of ________ cents or ________ dollar.

3. $6.19 means ________ dollars and ________ cents.

4. $5.26 means ________ dollars and ________ cents.

Add or subtract.

	a	b	c	d	e
5.	$45.63 − 32.91	54¢ 31¢ + 5¢	$59.61 5.03 + .17	$92.59 − 12.13	83¢ −64¢

Write the value of each collection.

6.

a

____

b

____

Compare the two sets of collections. Use "greater than," "less than," or "equal to."

7.

____

____

________ is ________ ________.

NAME ______________________

Check What You Learned

Money, Time, and Calendar

Determine the change for the following.

8. A book costs $3.48.

money value $ ________

cost of book − ________

change $ ________

Complete the following.

	a	b
9.	4:15 means ___ minutes after ___.	7:45 means ___ minutes to ___.
10.	12:55 means ___ minutes after ___.	12:55 means ___ minutes to ___.
11.	3:23 means ___ minutes after ___.	6:40 means ___ minutes to ___.

Tell the time to the nearest hour, half hour, quarter hour, or minute as indicated.

12.

a	b	c	d
hour	half hour	quarter hour	minute
___ : ___	___ : ___	___ : ___	___ : ___

Complete the following.

	a	b	c
13.	There are ____ hours in a day.	There are ____ months in a year.	There are ____ days in a leap year.
14.	There are ____ minutes in an hour.	There are ____ days in a week.	There are ____ days in a non-leap year.
15.	1 hour 33 minutes ____ minutes	70 minutes ____ hour 10 minutes	2 days 1 hour ____ hours

NAME ____________________

Check What You Know

Graphs and Probability

Use the picture graph to answer each question.

Students' Favorite Fruit

Apple	● ● ● ● ● ●
Orange	● ● ● ● ◖
Banana	● ● ● ● ● ●
Grape	● ●
Strawberry	● ● ● ◖
Peach	● ● ● ● ●

Key: ● = 2 students

1. Which fruit did the fewest students choose as their favorite? ________

2. Which 2 fruits did the most students choose as their favorite? ________

3. Seven students chose which fruit as their favorite? ________

4. How many students chose peach as their favorite fruit? ________

5. How many students chose orange as their favorite fruit? ________

Use the bar graph to answer each question.

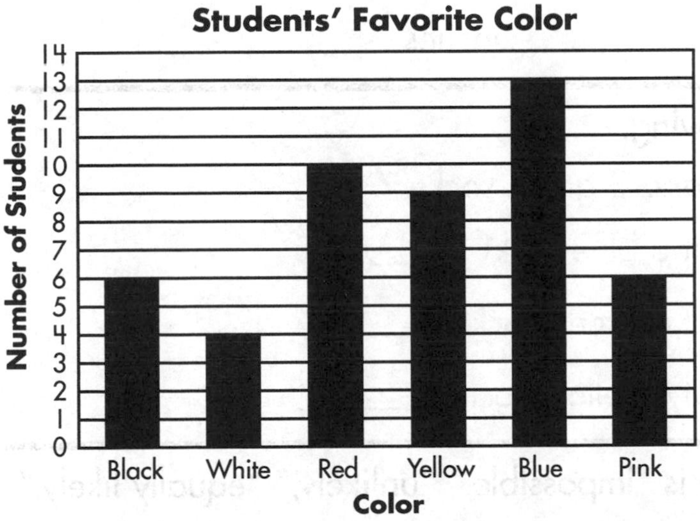

6. How many students chose red as their favorite color? ________

7. How many students chose yellow as their favorite color? ________

8. Which color did the fewest students choose as their favorite? ________

9. Which color did the most students choose as their favorite? ________

10. What is the difference between the blue and the white choices? ________

11. Six students chose which colors as their favorite? ____________________

12. Nine students chose which color as their favorite color? ____________

NAME ___________________________

CHAPTER 11 PRETEST

Check What You Know

Graphs and Probability

Use the line graph to answer each question.

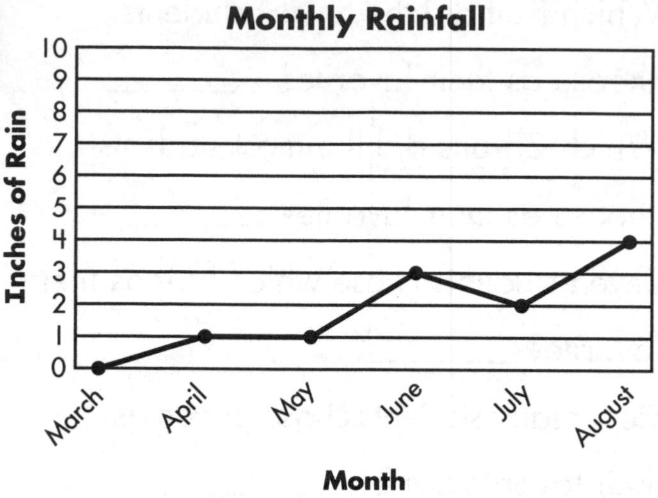

13. Which month had the most inches of rain? ________

14. Which month had the fewest inches of rain? ________

15. How many inches did it rain from March to August? ________

16. In which month did it rain 0 inches? ________

17. In which months did it rain 1 inch? ____________________

18. How many inches did it rain in June? ________ inches

19. How many inches did it rain in July? ________ inches

Write the correct probability for the following.

In a drawer you have 5 blue socks and 3 green socks.

20. What is the probability of pulling out a blue sock? ______

21. What is the probability of pulling out a green sock? ______

22. What is the probability of pulling out a yellow sock? ______

Indicate whether the probability outcome is "impossible," "unlikely," "equally likely," "likely," or "certain."

23. The outcome with a probability of $\frac{3}{4}$ is ____________________.

24. The outcome with a probability of $\frac{5}{5}$ is ____________________.

25. The outcome with a probability of $\frac{1}{8}$ is ____________________.

NAME ____________________

Lesson 11.1 Reading Picture Graphs

A **picture graph** uses symbols to represent data.

The key tells you the value of each symbol on the picture graph.

How many students have red hair color?

Students' Hair Color

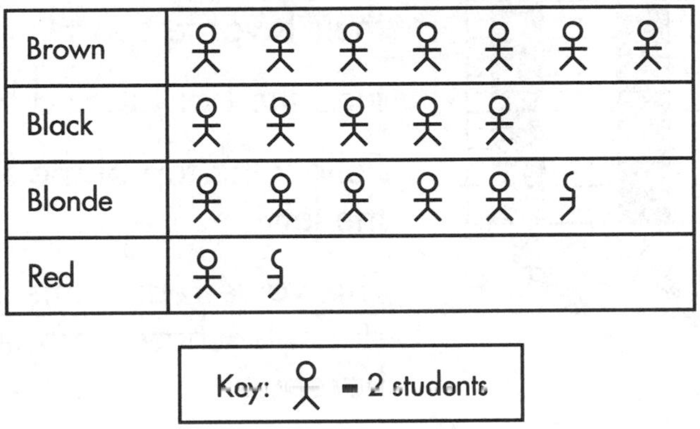
Brown
Black
Blonde
Red
Key:
= 2 students

Each stick figure represents two students.

Count by twos when counting the stick figures in the row labeled "red." Add 1 to the sum for the half stick figure.

__3__ students have red hair.

Use the picture graph to answer each question.

1. What hair color do the most students have? ____________

2. What hair color do the fewest students have? ____________

3. How many students have black hair? ____________

4. How many students have blonde hair? ____________

5. What hair color do 14 students have? ____________

NAME ____________________

Lesson 11.2 Reading Bar Graphs

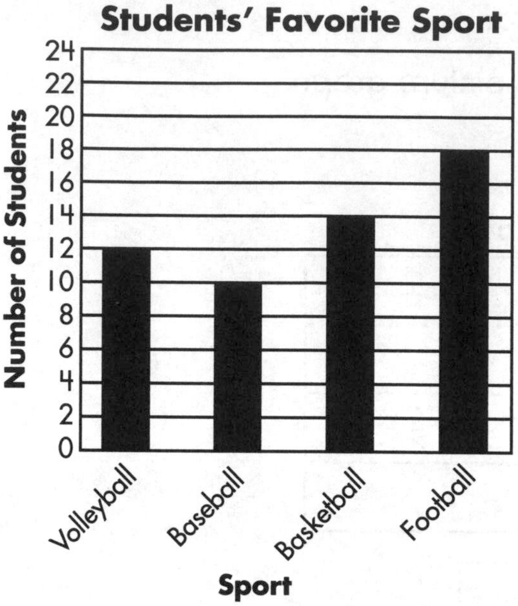

A **bar graph** uses rectangular bars to represent data.

The scale of a bar graph helps you identify the value of each bar.

How many students chose baseball as their favorite sport?

Find the bar labeled baseball.

Follow the top of the bar to the scale at the left.

This value represents the number of students whose favorite sport is baseball.

__10__ students chose baseball as their favorite sport.

Use the bar graph to answer each question.

1. Which sport did most students choose as their favorite? __________

2. Which sport did the fewest students choose as their favorite? __________

3. Which sport did 14 students choose as their favorite? __________

4. How many students chose volleyball as their favorite sport? __________

5. How many students chose football as their favorite sport? __________

6. What is the difference between the most favorite and the least favorite sport? __________

7. How many sports are recorded? __________

NAME ____________________

Lesson 11.3 Line Graphs

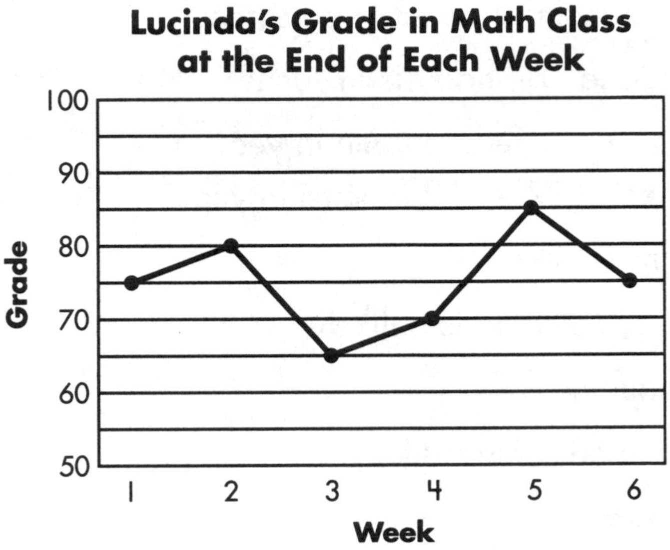

A **line graph** uses a line to show how data changes over a period of time.

Each point on the graph represents a data value at a given time.

What was Lucinda's grade in math class at the end of week 4?

Locate the point that represents the end of week 4. Follow this point to the scale at the left. This value represents Lucinda's grade at the end of week 4.

Lucinda had a grade of __70__ at the end of week 4.

Use the line graph to answer each question.

1. Which week was Lucinda's math grade the highest? ____________

2. Which week was Lucinda's math grade the lowest? ____________

3. What was Lucinda's week 1 grade? ____________

4. What was Lucinda's week 3 grade? ____________

5. Were the grades for any weeks the same? If so, which weeks? ____________

6. Which week did Lucinda have a math grade of 80? ____________

7. Which week did Lucinda have a math grade of 85? ____________

NAME ______________________

Lesson 11.4 Probability

Probability is the chance of an event occurring.

$$\text{Probability of an event} = \frac{\text{number of favorable outcomes}}{\text{total number of possible outcomes}}$$

What is the probability that Jane's birthday is in June?

$$\frac{\text{number of favorable outcomes}}{\text{total number of possible outcomes}} = \frac{1 \leftarrow \text{1 month in year}}{12 \leftarrow \text{12 months in year}}$$

If the probability is 0, then the outcome is impossible.

If the probability is between 0 and $\frac{1}{2}$, then the outcome is unlikely.

If the probability is $\frac{1}{2}$, then the outcome is equally likely.

If the probability is between $\frac{1}{2}$ and 1, then the outcome is likely.

If the probability is 1, then the outcome is certain.

What is the probability of

rolling a 7 on a 6-sided die?	rolling a 1 on a 6-sided die?	rolling a 1, 2, 3, or 4 on a 6-sided die?	rolling a 1, 2, 3, 4, 5, or 6 on a 6-sided die?
$\frac{0}{6} = 0$	$\frac{1}{6}$	$\frac{4}{6}$	$\frac{6}{6} = 1$
"impossible"	"unlikely"	"likely"	"certain"

Write the correct probability for the following. Indicate whether the outcome is "impossible," "unlikely," "equally likely," "likely," or "certain."

1. What is the probability of flipping a coin and getting a heads or tails? $\frac{2}{2}$ certain

2. What is the probability of flipping a coin and getting heads? ____ ________

3. What is the probability that Lenny's birthday is in a month starting with the letter M? (A calendar appears on p. 132.) ____ ________

4. What is the probability that Arnold's birthday is in a month that does *not* start with the letter J? ____ ________

5. What is the probability of rolling a 1, 3, 4, 5, or 6 on a six-sided die? ____ ________

NAME ______________________________

Check What You Learned

Graphs and Probability

Use the picture graph to answer each question.

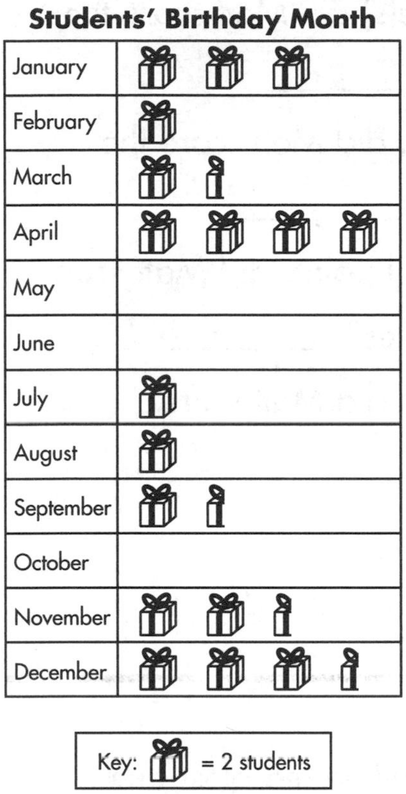
Students' Birthday Month
January
February
March
April
May
June
July
August
September
October
November
December
Key: = 2 students

1. In which month(s) are there no student birthdays? ______________________________

2. How many students have a birthday in January? ______

3. How many students have a birthday in July? ______

4. In which month do most students have their birthday? ______________

5. How many more students have their birthday in December than in September? ______________

6. Five students have their birthday in which month? ______________

7. Three students have their birthday in which month(s)? ______________

Use the bar graph to answer each question.

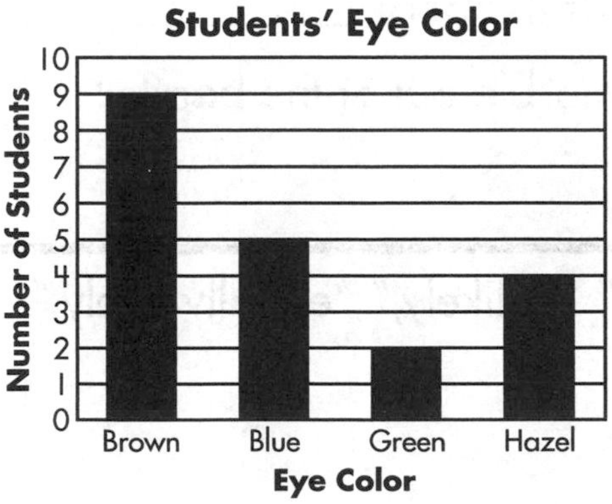
Students' Eye Color
Number of Students
0
1
2
3
4
5
6
7
8
9
10
Brown
Blue
Green
Hazel
Eye Color

8. How many students have blue eyes? ______

9. What eye color do most students have? ______

10. What eye color do the fewest students have? ______

11. Four students have what eye color? ______

12. Nine students have what eye color? ______

13. How many students have green eyes? ______

NAME ____________________

Check What You Learned

Graphs and Probability

Use the line graph to answer each question.

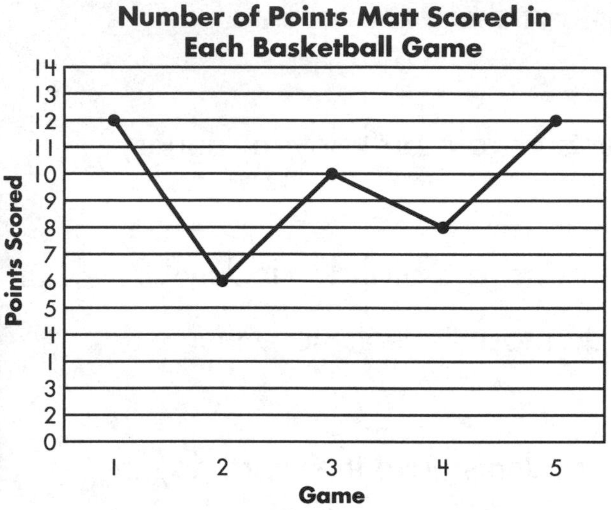

Number of Points Matt Scored in Each Basketball Game
Points Scored
14
13
12
11
10
9
8
7
6
5
4
1
3
2
0
1
2
3
4
5
Game

14. In which game(s) did Matt score the most points? 1-5

15. In which game did Matt score the fewest points? 6

16. How many total points did Matt score for all five games? 44

17. In which game did Matt score 6 points? ________

18. In which game did Matt score 10 points? ________

19. How many points did Matt score in game 1? ________

Write the correct probability for the following.

In a bag, there are 3 red marbles, 6 blue marbles, 2 white marbles, and 1 black marble.

20. What is the probability of pulling a blue marble out of the bag? ________

21. What is the probability of pulling a red marble out of the bag? ________

22. What is the probability of pulling a white or black marble out of the bag?

____

Indicate whether the probability outcome is "impossible," "unlikely," "equally likely," "likely," or "certain."

23. The outcome with a probability of $\frac{6}{6}$ is ________.

24. The outcome with a probability of $\frac{0}{3}$ is ________.

25. The outcome with a probability of $\frac{5}{6}$ is ________.

CHAPTER 11 POSTTEST

NAME ______________________

Check What You Know

Geometry

Match each figure in column a with its name in column b.

a

1. ________ 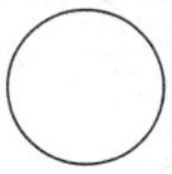

2. ________ 

3. ________ 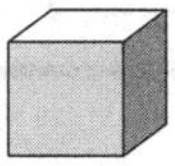

4. ________ 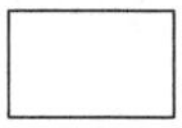

5. ________ 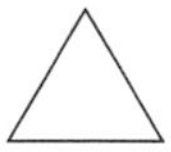

6. ________ 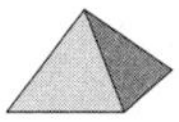

7. ________ 

b

A. circle
B. cube
C. rectangle
D. sphere
E. square
F. square pyramid
G. triangle

Label each figure as solid or plane.

8.

a  ________

b 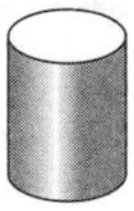 ________

c 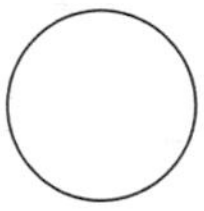 ________

d 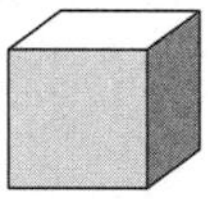 ________

e 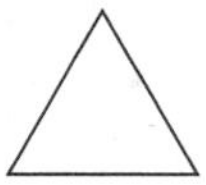 ________

Complete each table.

	Figure	Number of Sides	Number of Square Corners	Number of Other Corners		Figure	Number of Square Faces	Number of Triangle Faces	Number of Rectangle Faces	Number of Edges
9.	square				**12.**	cube				
10.	circle				**13.**	square pyramid				
11.	rectangle				**14.**	sphere				

NAME ______________________

Check What You Know

Geometry

Indicate if the figures are congruent or not congruent.

15. **a** **b** **c** **d**

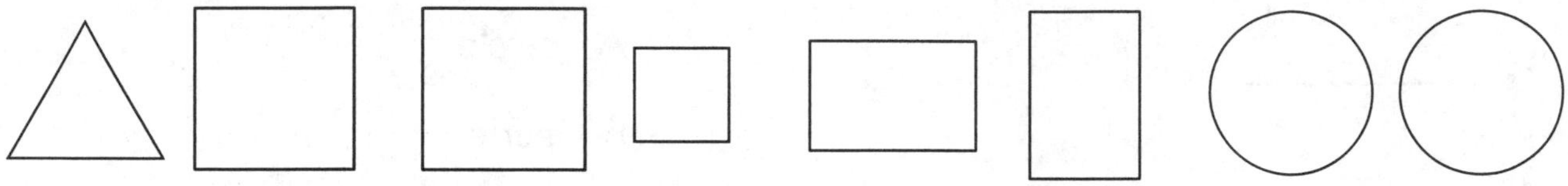

______ ______ ______ ______

Indicate if the objects are not symmetrical or symmetrical. If the object is symmetrical, draw the line of symmetry.

16. **a** **b** **c** **d**

______ ______ ______ ______

Is the line drawn on each figure a line of symmetry?

17. **a** **b** **c** **d**

______ ______ ______ ______

Identify each figure as a point, line, line segment, ray, or angle. Name each figure.

18. **a** **b** **c** **d**

______ ______ ______ ______

______ ______ ______ ______

Lesson 12.1 Plane Figures

A **plane figure** is a flat surface.

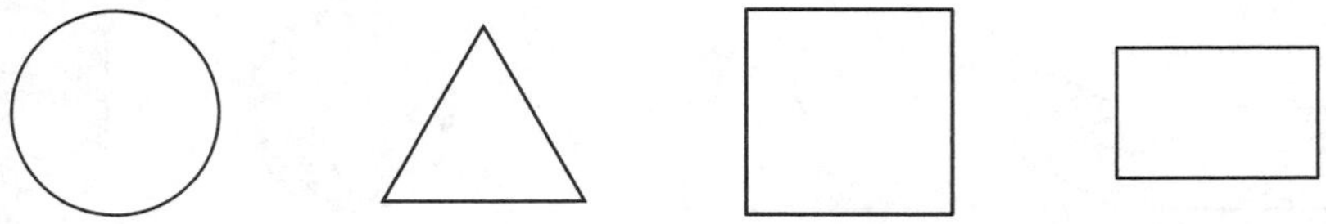

circle | triangle | square | rectangle

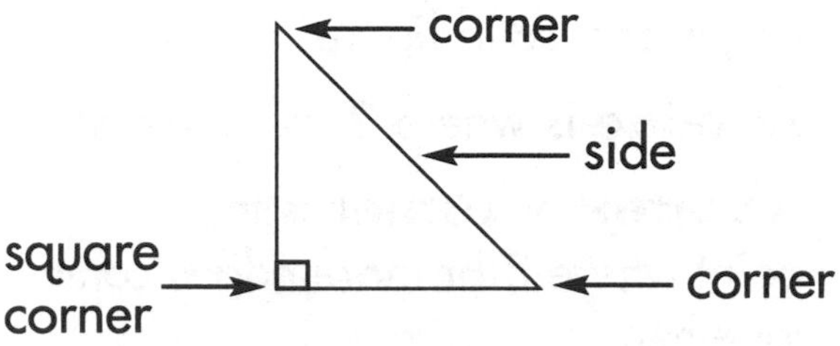

Each side of a triangle, square, and rectangle is a **line segment**.

The point where two line segments meet is a **corner** or a **square corner**.

A square corner is a right angle. A right angle has a measure of 90°.

Draw the following plane figures.

	a	b	c	d
1.	triangle	rectangle	square	circle

Complete the following.

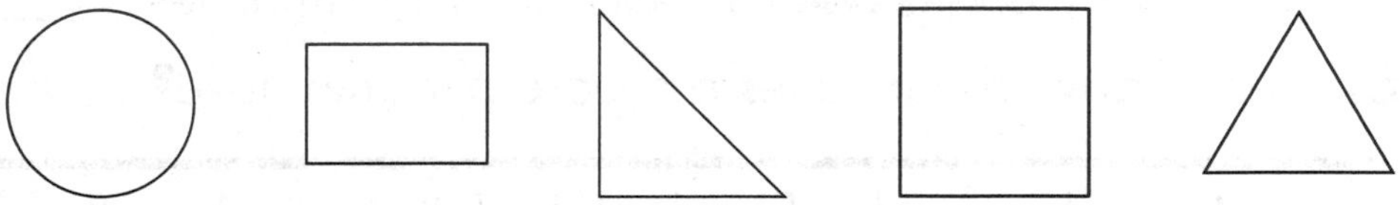

	a	b	c	d	e
2. number of sides	0				
3. number of square corners			1		0
4. number of other corners					

Lesson 12.2 Solid Figures

A **solid figure** is a three-dimensional object. Solid figures may be hollow or solid.

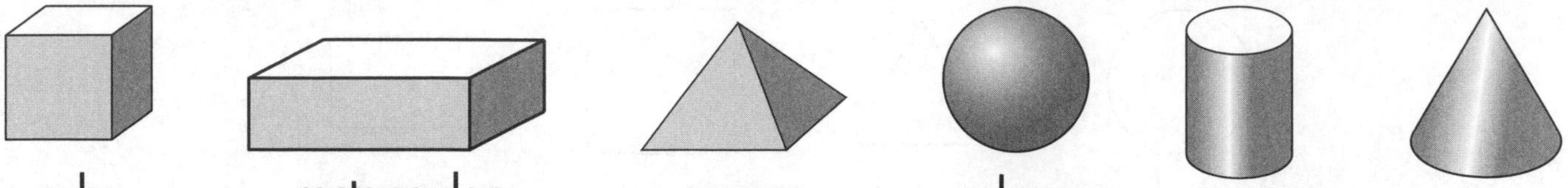

cube | rectangular prism | square pyramid | sphere | cylinder | cone

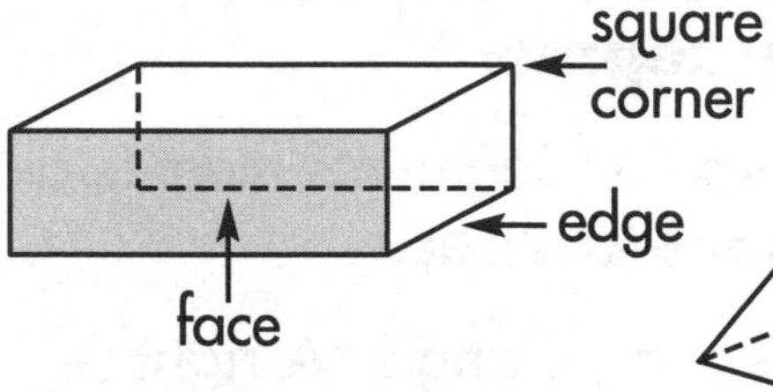

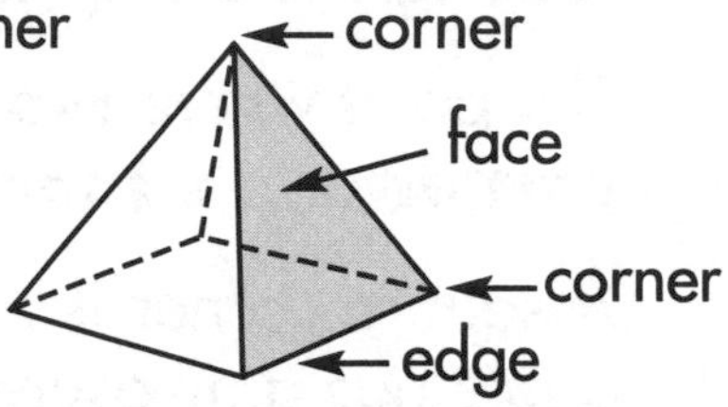

A **face** is the shape formed by the edges of a solid figure.

An **edge** is where 2 faces intersect.

A **vertex** or **corner** is the point where 3 or more edges come together.

Complete the table.

	Solid Figure	Number of Square Faces	Number of Rectangle Faces	Number of Triangle Faces
1.	cube			0
2.	rectangular prism			
3.	square pyramid	1		

4. How many edges does a sphere have? _____ edges

5. How many edges does a square pyramid have? _____ edges

6. How many edges does a cube have? _____ edges

7. How many edges does a rectangular prism have? _____ edges

8. How many corners does a square pyramid have? _____ corners

Give a physical example of each of the following plane figures.

	a	b	c
9.	cube sugar cube	rectangular prism __________	square pyramid __________
10.	sphere __________	cylinder __________	cone __________

NAME ____________________

Lesson 12.3 Comparing Figures

Label each the figure as plane or solid.

	a	b	c	d
1.	 solid	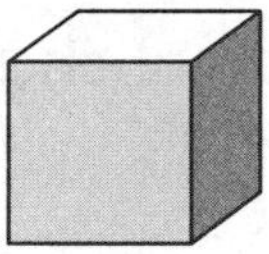 ______	 ______	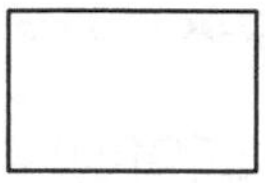 ______
2.	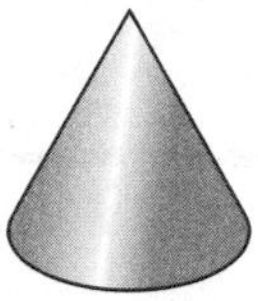 ______	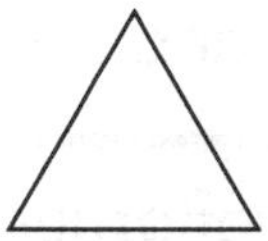 ______	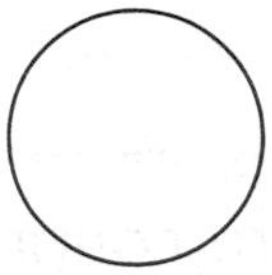 ______	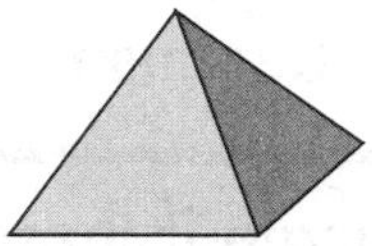 ______

Match the solid figures with the plane figures that are shaped most like them. Answers may be used more than once.

___B___ **3.** 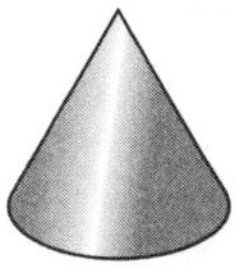

______ **4.** 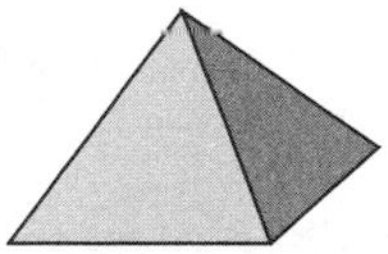

______ **5.** 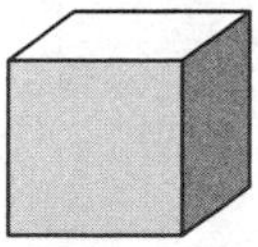

______ **6.** 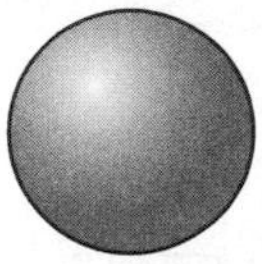

______ **7.** 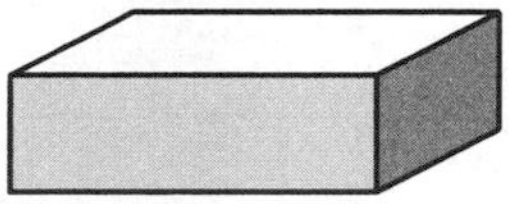

______ **8.** 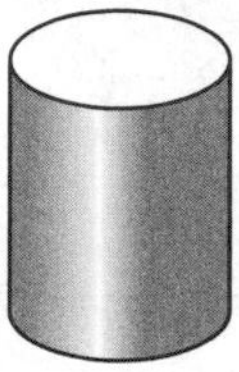

A. 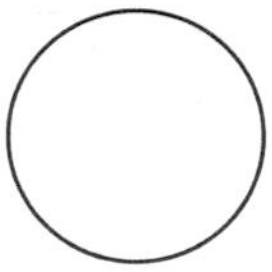

B. 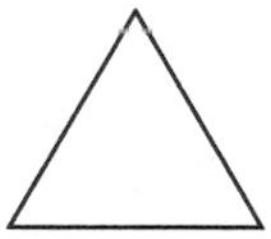

C. 

D. 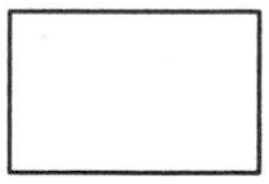

NAME ______________________

Lesson 12.4 Congruent Shapes

Congruent figures have exactly the same shape and size.

Is a  congruent to a  ? Why or why not?

No, because a square and a triangle are different shapes.

Is 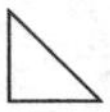 congruent to  ? Why or why not?

No, because the two triangles are not exactly the same shape.

Is  congruent to  ? Why or why not?

Yes, because they are exactly the same shape and size.

Indicate if these figures are congruent or not congruent.

a b c d

1. 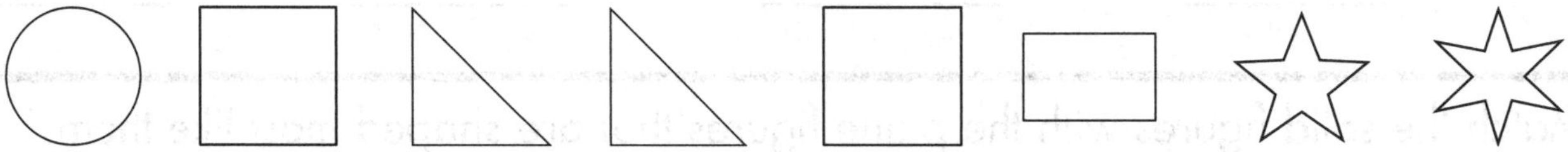

not congruent ______ ______ ______

2. 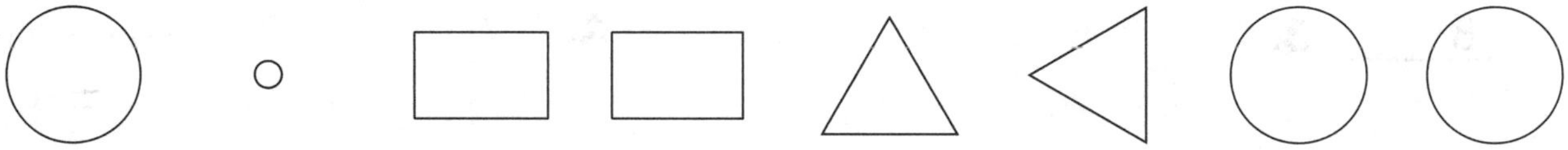

______ ______ ______ ______

3. 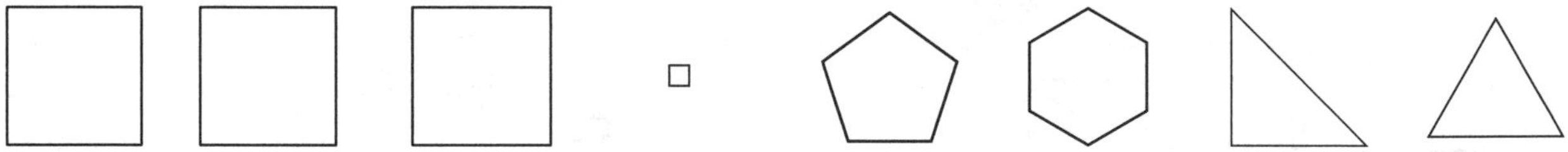

______ ______ ______ ______

4. 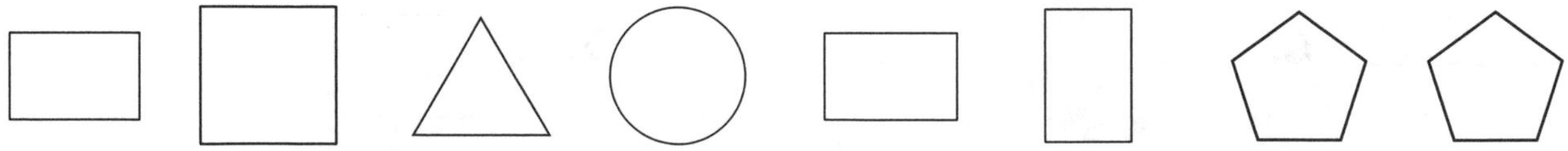

______ ______ ______ ______

5. 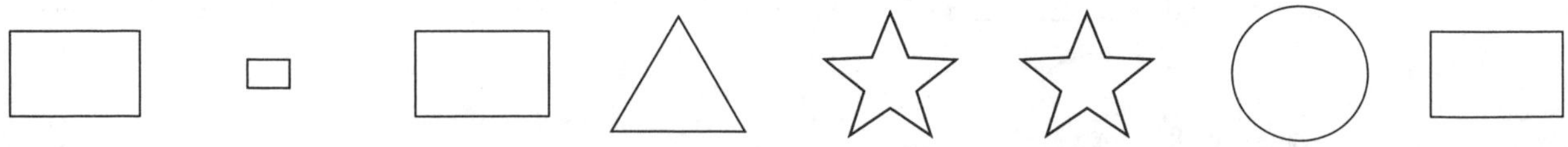

______ ______ ______ ______

NAME ______________________

Lesson 12.5 Symmetrical Shapes

A figure or a shape is **symmetrical** when one-half of the figure is the mirror image of the other half.

A **line of symmetry** divides a figure or shape into two halves that are congruent.

The letter A is symmetrical.

The letter A has one line of symmetry.

The letter O is symmetrical.

The letter O has many lines of symmetry.

The letter F is not symmetrical.

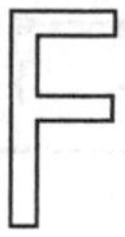

The letter F does not have a line of symmetry.

Is the line drawn on each figure a line of symmetry?

1.

a 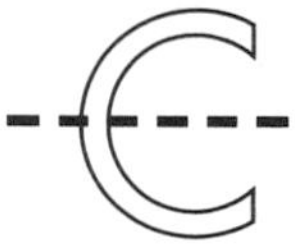 ________

b  ________

c  ________

d  no

2.

a  ________

b  ________

c  no

d 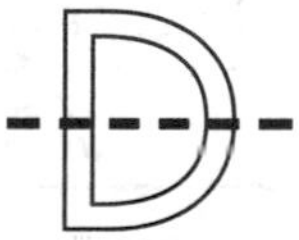 ________

Label each figure as not symmetrical or symmetrical. If the figure is symmetrical, draw the line (or lines) of symmetry.

3.

a 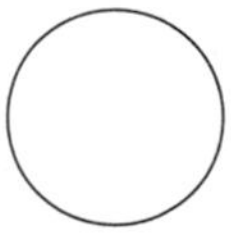 ________

b  ________

c  ________

d  ________

4.

a  ________

b  ________

c 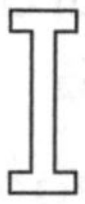 ________

d  ________

NAME ____________________

Lesson 12.6 Line Segments

	Figure	Definition	Dimension	How to Name Each Figure
point	• A	An exact location in space.	no length no width	A, capital letter
line	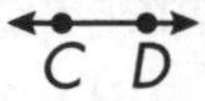	A collection of points going on and on in both directions. Arrowheads indicate infinite length.	length no width	$\overleftrightarrow{CD}$
line segment	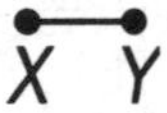	A part of a line. Two endpoints and the collection of points between the endpoints.	length no width	$\overline{XY}$
ray		A part of a line. One endpoint and the rest of the line that goes on and on.	length no width	$\overrightarrow{FG}$

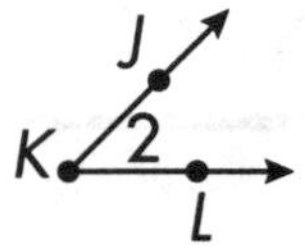

An **angle** is formed by two rays with a common endpoint. This endpoint is called a **vertex**. This angle is named ∠JKL, ∠K, or ∠2. Angles are found wherever lines and line segments intersect.

Identify each figure as a point, line, line segment, ray, or angle. Name each figure.

1.

a 

line segment
$\overline{AB}$

b • P
point
P

c • Q

d 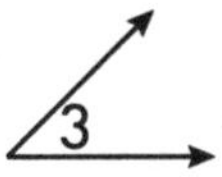

e 

2.

a 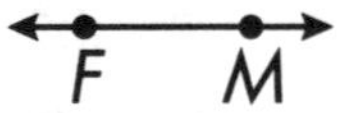

b 

c 

d 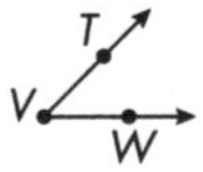

e 

Identify the parts of this angle.

3. The vertex is point __________.

4. $\overrightarrow{XY}$ is a __________.

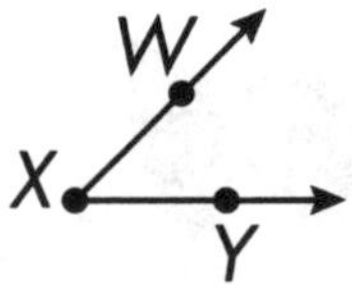

Use a ruler, if necessary, to draw these items.

	a	b	c	d	e
5.	line	line segment	ray	angle	point

NAME ____________________

Check What You Learned

Geometry

Name each figure. Label each figure as solid or plane.

	a	b	c	d
1.	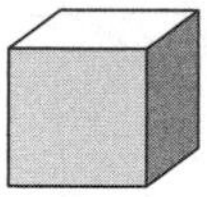	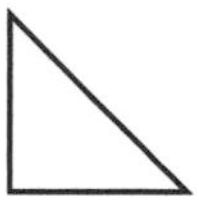	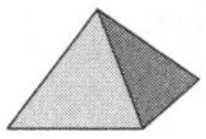	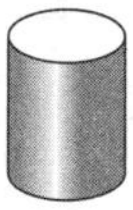
	____________ ____________	____________ ____________	____________ ____________	____________ ____________
2.	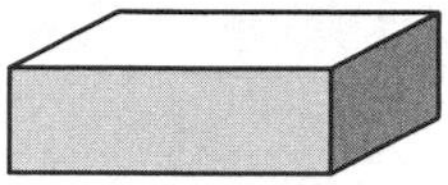	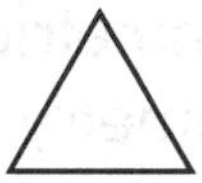	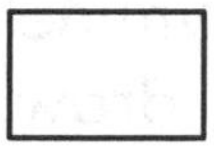	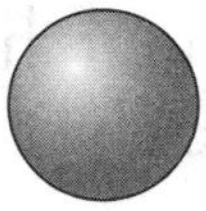
	____________ ____________	____________ ____________	____________ ____________	____________ ____________
3.		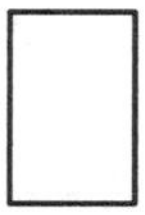	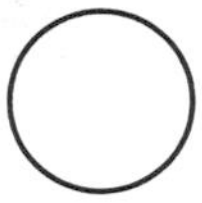	
	____________ ____________	____________ ____________	____________ ____________	____________ ____________

How many sides or edges are there on these figures?

	a	b	c	d
4.		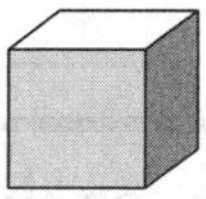	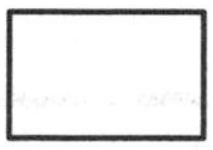	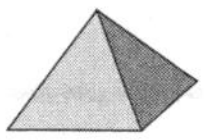
	____________	____________	____________	____________

How many faces are on each figure?

	a	b	c	d
5.		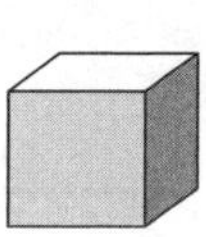	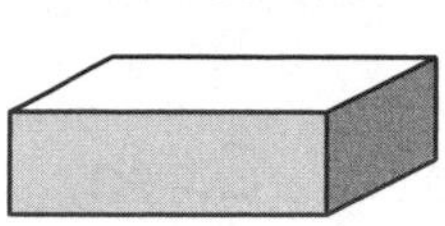	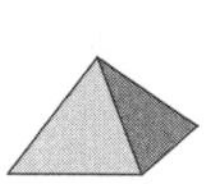
	____________	____________	____________	____________

Check What You Learned

Geometry

Indicate if the figures are congruent or not congruent.

6.

a 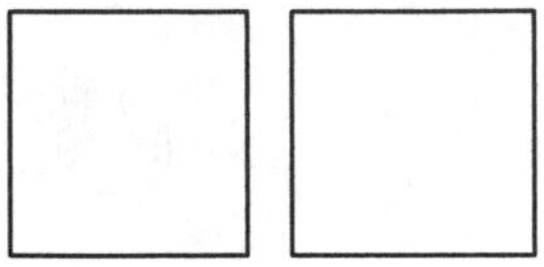 ____________

b 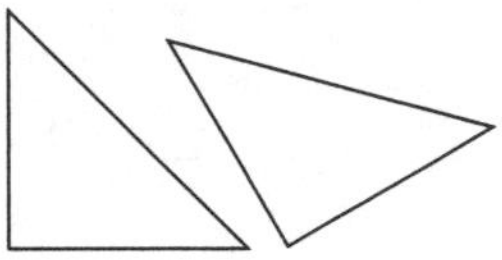 ____________

c 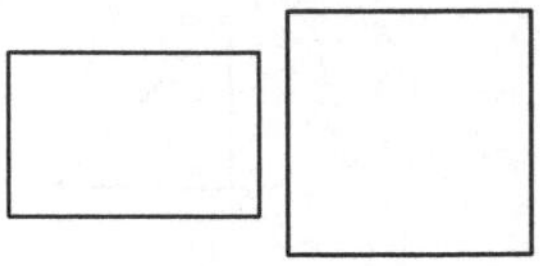 ____________

d 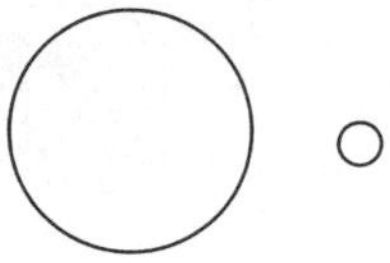 ____________

Indicate if the objects are symmetrical or not symmetrical.
If the object is symmetrical, draw the line of symmetry.

7.

a  ____________

b  ____________

c 

____

d 

____

Is the line drawn on each figure a line of symmetry?

8.

a 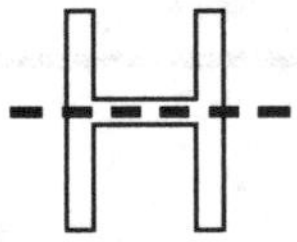

____

b 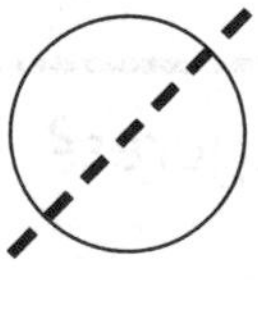 ____________

c 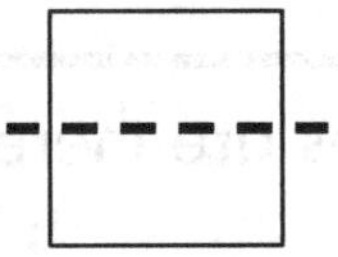 ____________

d 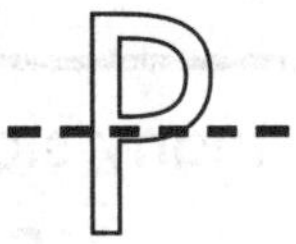

____

Match each figure with its description.

9. ______ 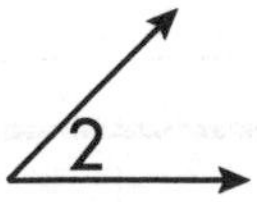

A. point

10. ______ 

B. angle

11. ______ 

C. ray

12. ______ 

D. line

Match each figure with its name.

13. ______ 

G. $\angle GHJ$

14. ______ 

H. $\overline{AB}$

15. ______ 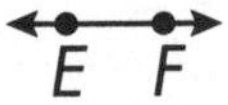

I. $\overrightarrow{CD}$

16. ______ 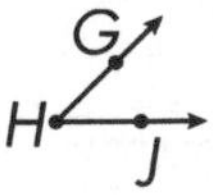

J. $\overleftrightarrow{EF}$

NAME ____________________

Check What You Know

Preparing for Algebra

Complete the pattern.

1.

______

______

______

Write the number of objects under each group of objects.

	a	b	c	d	e
2.	○ ○	○ ○ ○ ○	○ ○	○ ○ ○ ○	○ ○
	______	______	______	______	______
3.	△ △ △ △ △	△ △ △ △	△ △ △	△ △	△
	______	______	______	______	______
4.	□	□ □ □	□ □ □ □ □	□ □ □ □ □ □ □	□ □ □ □ □ □ □ □ □
	______	______	______	______	______

Complete the pattern by using addition or subtraction.

				a	b	c	d
5.	30	26	22	____	____	____	____
6.	1	2	3	____	____	____	____
7.	5	10	15	____	____	____	____
8.	4	8	16	____	____	____	____
9.	1	3	5	____	____	____	____
10.	10	9	8	____	____	____	____

NAME ____________________

Check What You Know

Preparing for Algebra

Complete each repeating geometric pattern.

		a	b	c
11.		______	______	______
12.		______	______	______
13.	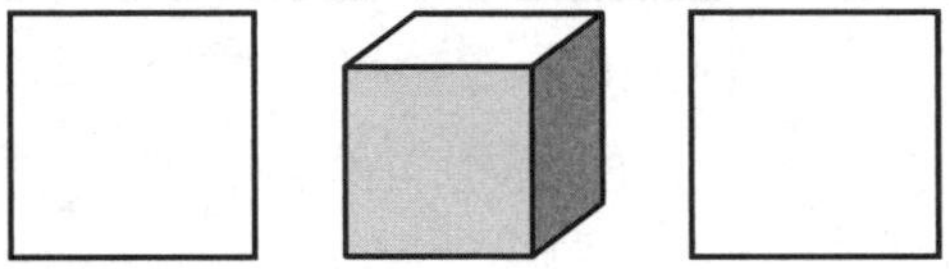	______	______	______

Complete the following.

	a	b	c	d
14.	$3 + \square = 3$	$5 + 0 = \square$	$7 \times 1 = \square$	$\square \times 1 = 6$
15.	$5 + 4 = 9$ or $5 + 4 = 2 + \square$	$6 + 9 = 15$ or $6 + 9 = 10 + \square$	$2 \times 9 = 18$ or $2 \times 9 = 6 \times \square$	$4 \times 5 = 20$ or $4 \times 5 = 10 \times \square$

Write the number sentence. For the missing part, use a box ($\square$). Solve each number sentence.

16. The sum of two and three is what number? ____________

The sum of the two and three is ____________.

17. The product of five and four is what number? ____________

The product of five and four is ____________.

18. Ten minus eight is what number? ____________

Ten minus eight is ____________.

NAME ______________________

Lesson 13.1 Patterns

Start at the top of each column and work down. Complete each pattern.

1.

2.

3.

4.

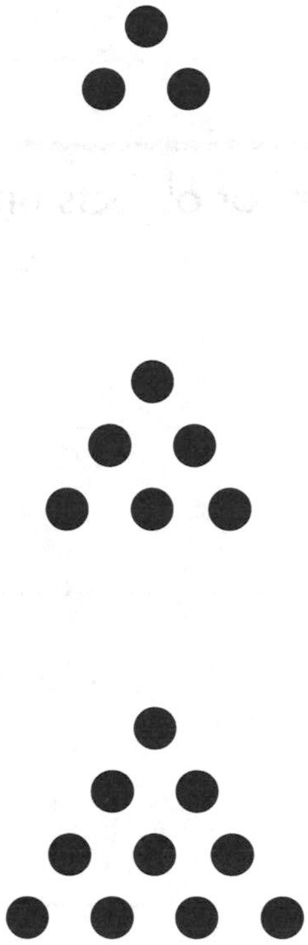

5.

NAME ______________________

Lesson 13.2 Transferring Patterns

1 2 3 4 5

Write the number of objects under each group of objects in each pattern.

	a	b	c	d	e

1.

_____ _____ _____ _____ _____

2.

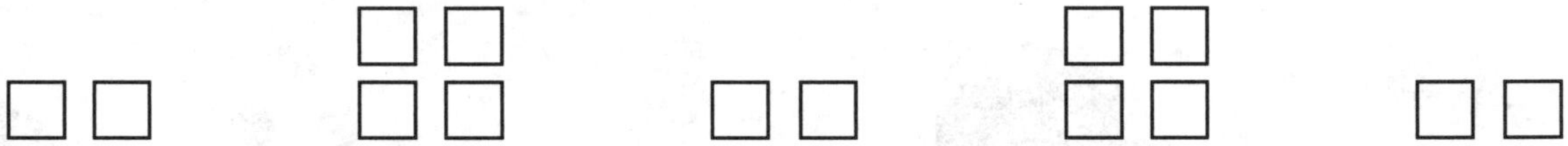

_____ _____ _____ _____ _____

3.

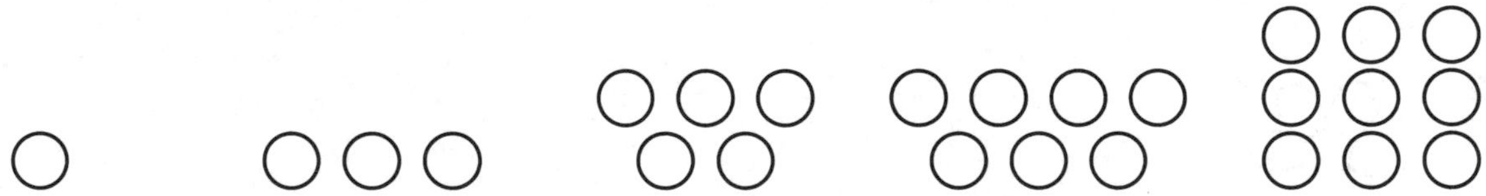

_____ _____ _____ _____ _____

4.

_____ _____ _____ _____ _____

5.

_____ _____ _____ _____ _____

NAME ______________________

Lesson 13.3 Number Patterns

A number pattern can be developed by addition or subtraction.

Complete this pattern by subtraction.

25 − 5 = 20   20 − 5 = 15   15 − 5 = 10   10 − 5 = 5   5 − 5 = 0

25   20   15   10   5   0

Complete the pattern by using addition or subtraction.

				a	b	c
1.	2	4	6	8	10	12
2.	1	3	5	____	____	____
3.	20	18	16	____	____	____
4.	21	15	10	____	____	____
5.	13	12	11	____	____	____
6.	5	10	15	____	____	____
7.	3	6	9	____	____	____
8.	10	20	40	____	____	____
9.	16	13	10	____	____	____
10.	10	9	8	____	____	____

NAME ______________________

Lesson 13.4 Geometric Patterns

Complete each repeating geometric pattern.

a b c

1. 

2. 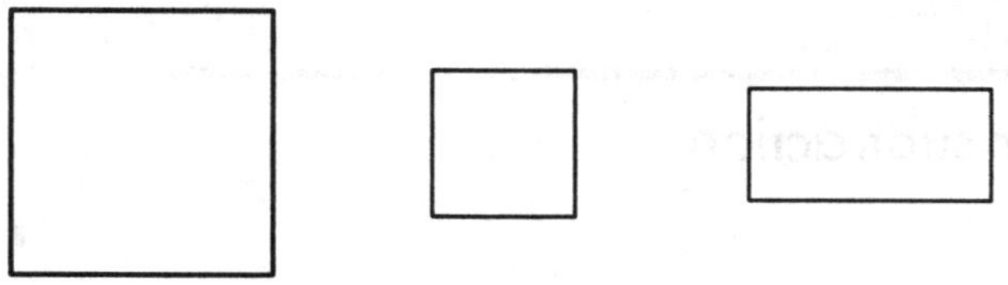

3. 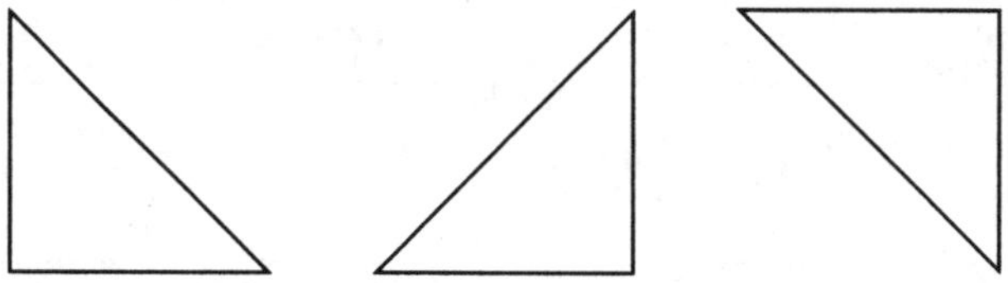

4. 

5. 

6. 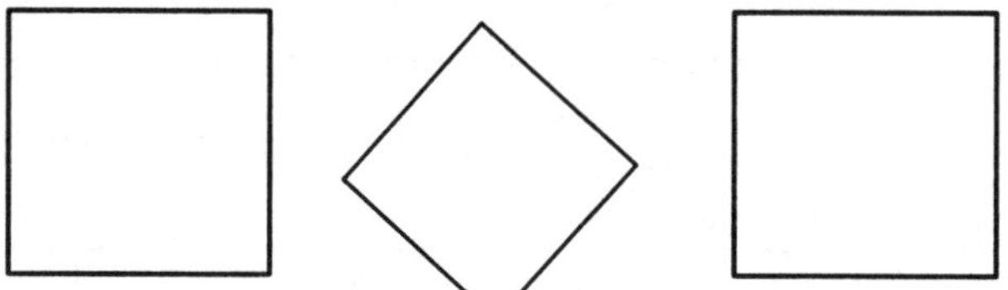

7. 

8. 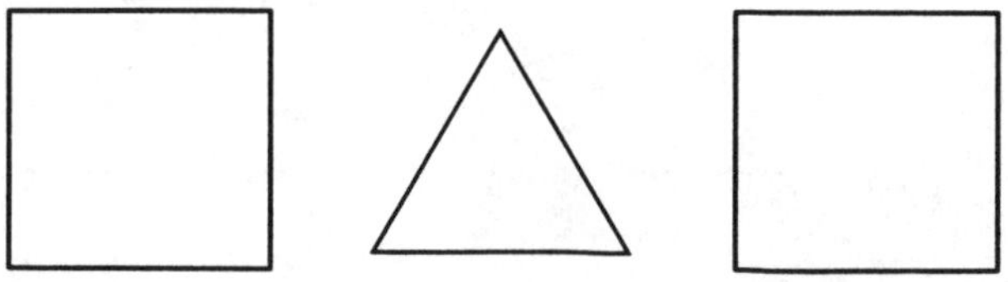

NAME ______________________

Lesson 13.5 Number Sentences

A **number sentence** is an equation with numbers.

Identity Property		**Commutative Property**	
for addition:	0 + 3 = 3	for addition:	3 + 2 = 2 + 3
for multiplication:	1 × 3 = 3	for multiplication:	4 × 2 = 2 × 4

A number sentence can change its look but not change its value.

3 + 5 = 8 or 3 + 5 = 4 + 4　　　3 × 8 = 24 or 3 × 8 = 6 × 4

Complete each number sentence.

	a	b	c	d
1.	0 + 4 = [4]	0 + 6 = □	□ + 2 = 2	□ + 7 = 7
2.	1 × 2 = □	1 × 5 = □	□ × 4 = 4	□ × 9 = 9
3.	7 + 2 = □ + 7	3 + 4 = □ + 3	1 + 2 = 2 + □	□ + 5 = 5 + 4
4.	5 × 7 = 7 × □	4 × □ = 3 × 4	□ × 3 = 3 × 5	9 × 4 = □ × 9

Complete the following.

	a	b	c	d
5.	2 + 7 = 9 or 2 + 7 = 5 + [4]	5 + 7 = 12 or 5 + 7 = 6 + □	4 + 3 = 7 or 4 + 3 = 5 + □	6 + 9 = 15 or 6 + 9 = 10 + □
6.	6 + 4 = 10 or 6 + 4 = 5 + □	6 + 7 = 13 or 6 + 7 = 8 + □	5 + 3 = 8 or 5 + 3 = 6 + □	9 + 2 = 11 or 9 + 2 = 5 + □
7.	5 × 6 = 30 or 5 × 6 = 10 × [3]	4 × 3 = 12 or 4 × 3 = 2 × □	6 × 3 = 18 or 6 × 3 = 9 × □	6 × 2 = 12 or 6 × 2 = 4 × □

NAME ______________________

Lesson 13.5 Problem Solving

Math Symbol	Key Words
$=$	is, is equal to, equals
$+$	added to, sum, and, plus
$-$	subtracted from, difference, minus
$\times$	multiplied by, the product of, times
$\div$	divided by

Write each number sentence. Put a box ($\square$) in the sentence for the missing part. Solve each number sentence.

1. The sum of two and three is what number? $2 + 3 = \boxed{5}$

The sum of the two and three is five.

2. Seven minus two is what number? __________

Seven minus two is __________.

3. Four times three is what number? __________

Four times three is __________.

4. Fourteen divided by two is what number? __________

Fourteen divided by two is __________.

5. Five added to what number is seven? __________

Five added to __________ is seven.

6. Thirteen minus what number is ten? __________

Thirteen minus __________ is ten.

NAME ______________________

Check What You Learned

Preparing for Algebra

Complete the pattern.

1.

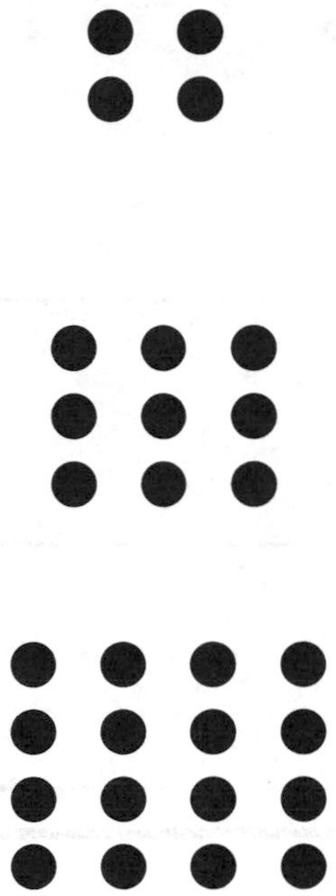

______

______

______

Write the number of objects under each group.

	a	b	c	d	e
2.	○	○ ○	○ ○ ○	○ ○ ○ ○	○ ○ ○ ○ ○
	____	____	____	____	____
3.	△△△△△ △△△△△	△△△△ △△△△	△△△ △△△	△△ △△	△ △
	____	____	____	____	____
4.	□□□□□ □□□□□	□□□□□ □□□□	□□□□ □□□	□□ □□	
	____	____	____	____	____

Complete the pattern by using addition or subtraction.

				a	b	c	d
5.	1	2	3	____	____	____	____
6.	50	45	40	____	____	____	____
7.	100	90	80	____	____	____	____
8.	4	8	12	____	____	____	____
9.	2	4	6	____	____	____	____
10.	33	35	37	____	____	____	____

CHAPTER 13 POSTTEST

NAME ____________________

Check What You Learned

Preparing for Algebra

Complete each repeating geometric pattern.

		a	b	c
11.		________	________	________
12.	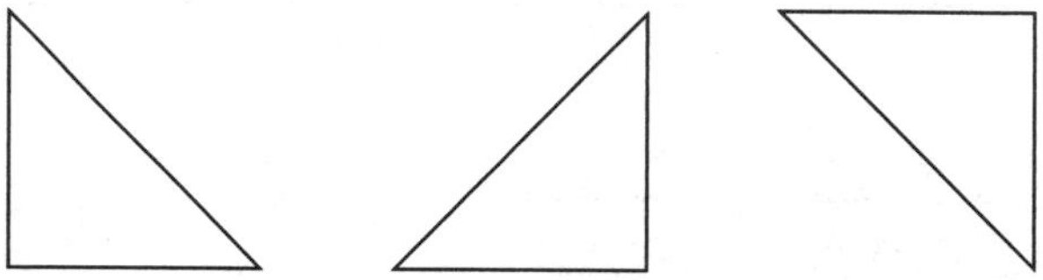	________	________	________
13.		________	________	________

Complete the following.

	a	b	c	d
14.	5 + ☐ = 5	☐ + 0 = 4	2 × 1 = ☐	3 × 1 = ☐
15.	2 + 7 = 9 or 2 + 7 = 6 + ☐	5 + 9 = 14 or 5 + 9 = 8 + ☐	3 × 8 = 24 or 3 × 8 = 4 × ☐	6 × 2 = 12 or 6 × 2 = 4 × ☐

Write each number sentence. For the missing part, use a box (☐). Solve each number sentence.

16. Twelve divided by six is what number? __________

Twelve divided by six is __________.

17. Seven times three is what number? __________

Seven times three is __________.

18. Five plus six is what number? __________

Five plus six is __________.

NAME ____________________

Final Test Chapters 1–13

Add or subtract.

	a	b	c	d	e
1.	9 +4	3 +19	21 +42	67 +29	57 + 4
2.	319 23 +152	59 63 +142	57 59 +63	403 +907	500 +320
3.	23 −11	54 −19	316 − 23	594 − 95	419 − 21
4.	113 − 92	54 −13	8 −7	46 −32	511 − 21
5.	1321 +4923	6876 + 192	541 +962	5921 +2543	3864 + 193
6.	4321 − 491	5963 −1892	9876 −7293	5434 − 502	4732 −1693

SHOW YOUR WORK

Solve each problem.

7. In 1984, Mr. Alvin was 103 years old. What year was he born?

Mr. Alvin was born in __________.

8. Sandy spent 14 dollars of her 38 dollars on a radio. How much money does she have left?

Sandy has __________ dollars left.

7.

8.

CHAPTERS 1–13 FINAL TEST

NAME ____________________

Final Test Chapters 1–13

Round each number to the place named.

	a	b	c	d
9.	4,932 tens	59,651 hundreds	596 hundreds	720 hundreds

Write each number in expanded form.

	a	b	c	d
10.	593	400,430	50,603	5,964

Compare each pair of numbers. Write <, >, or =.

	a	b	c	d
11.	5 ___ 7	4 ___ 4	21 ___ 27	154 ___ 151

Multiply or divide.

	a	b	c	d	e
12.	3×4	52×5	42×3	7×8	61×2
13.	54×3	92×1	13×5	4×5	16×3
14.	$8\overline{)64}$	$6\overline{)24}$	$9\overline{)54}$	$4\overline{)12}$	$5\overline{)5}$
15.	$7\overline{)21}$	$4\overline{)20}$	$3\overline{)6}$	$6\overline{)18}$	$2\overline{)10}$

NAME ______________________

Final Test Chapters 1–13

SHOW YOUR WORK

Solve each problem.

16. There are 27 students in the classroom. Each math student receives 3 papers. How many total papers are there?

There are a total of __________ papers.

17. There are 64 seats in the movie theater. There are 8 rows. If the same number of seats are in each row, how many seats are in each row?

There are __________ seats in each row.

16.

17.

What fraction of each figure or set is shaded?

18. a b c d

__________ __________ __________ __________

What fraction of each figure is shaded? Compare the fractions. Use >, <, or =.

19. a b c

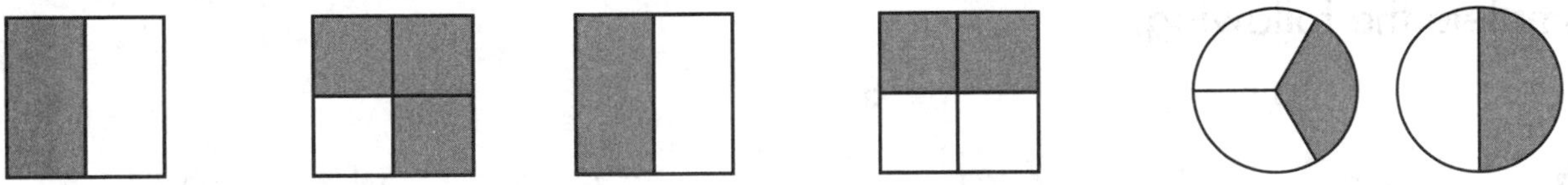

___ ◯ ___ ___ ◯ ___ ___ ◯ ___

20.

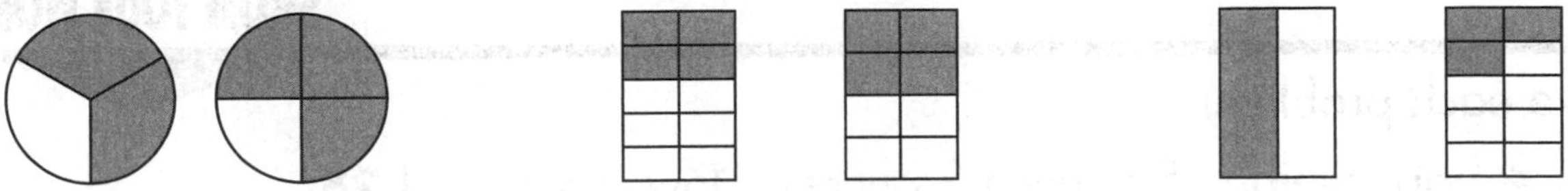

___ ◯ ___ ___ ◯ ___ ___ ◯ ___

NAME ____________________

Final Test Chapters 1–13

Use a ruler to find the measure of each rectangle.

21. Measure to the nearest inch. ______ in.

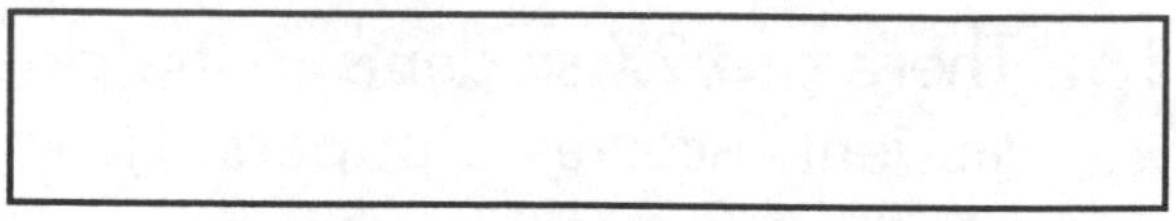

22. Measure to the nearest centimeter. ______ cm

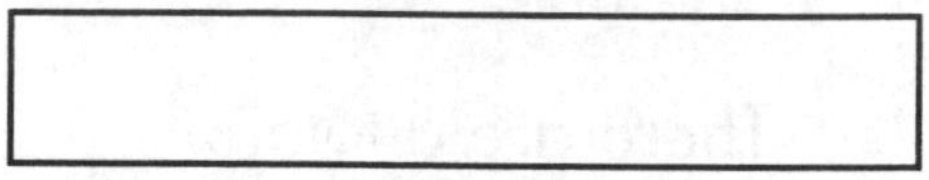

Complete the following.

	a	b	c
23.	500 cm = ______ m	5,000 g = ______ kg	6,000 mg = ______ g
24.	6,000 mL = ______ L	3 g = ______ mg	7 m = ______ cm

What is the temperature reading on each thermometer?

25.

a

______ °C

b

______ °F

c

______ °C ______ °F

Complete the following.

	a	b	c	d
26.	3 ft. = ___ in.	2 yd. = ___ ft.	4 c. = ___ pt.	16 pt. = ___ gal.
27.	5 gal. = ___ qt.	12 c. = ___ qt.	2 pt. = ___ c.	2 ft. = ___ in.

SHOW YOUR WORK

Solve each problem.

28. A baby weighs 5 pounds 2 ounces. How much does the baby weigh in ounces?

The baby weighs __________ ounces.

28.

NAME ____________________

Final Test Chapters 1–13

Complete the following.

29. 15 pennies have a value of ________ cents or ________ nickels.

30. 75 pennies have a value of ________ cents or ________ quarters.

31. $7.52 means ________ dollars and ________ cents.

Determine the change for the following.

32. A radio costs $5.72.

money value	$ ________
cost of radio	− ________
change	$ ________

Complete the following.

	a	b
33.	7:42 means ___ minutes after ___.	7:42 means ___ minutes to ___.

Write the time to the nearest hour, half hour, quarter hour, or minute as indicated.

34.

a	b	c	d
hour	half hour	quarter hour	minute
___ : ___	___ : ___	___ : ___	___ : ___

heads	● ● ● ● ● ◖
tails	● ● ● ●

Key: ● = 2 students

Use this picture graph to answer the following questions.

35. How many students had heads? ______

36. How many students had tails? ______

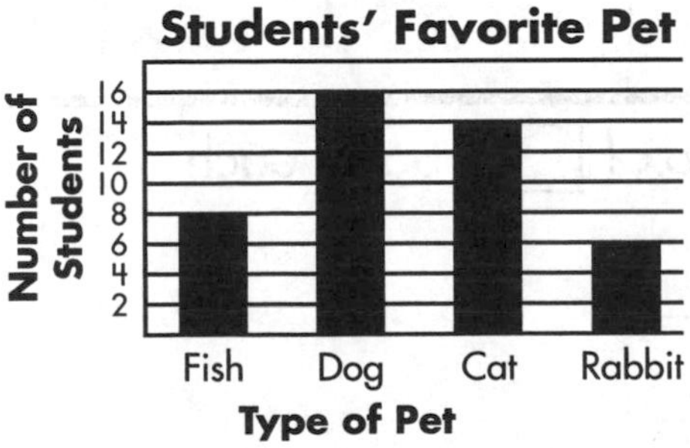

Use this bar graph to answer the following questions.

37. Which pet did the most students choose? ______

38. Which pet did the fewest students choose? ______

NAME ____________________

Final Test Chapters 1–13

Troy's Tips for Each Day for 1 Week

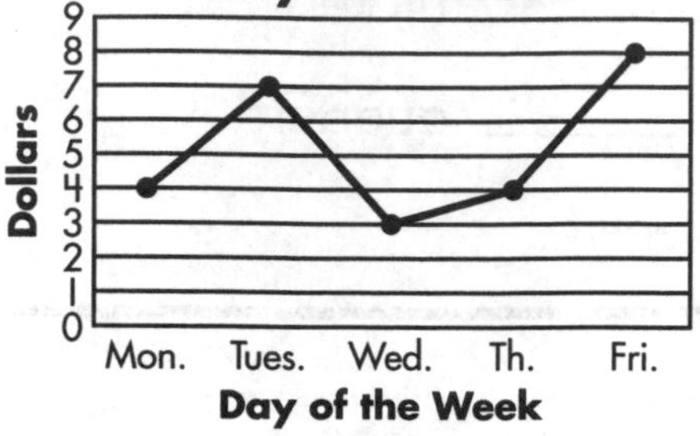

Use the line graph to answer questions 39–41.

39. What day of the week did Troy receive the most tips? ________

40. Troy received exactly 4 dollars on which days? ________

41. What is the total amount of tips that Troy received for the week? ________

Name each figure. Label each as solid or plane.

42.

a  ________ ________

b  ________ ________

c 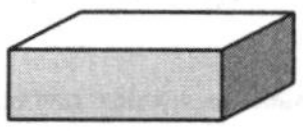 ________ ________

d 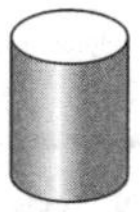 ________ ________

Name each figure.

43.

a ________

b ________

c ________

d 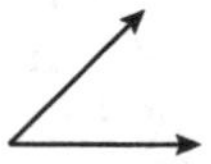 ________

Complete the pattern.

44. 20 25 30 a ___ b ___ 13 11 9 c ___ d ___

Complete the following.

45. a $3 + 0 = \square$ b $5 \times 1 = \square$ c $5 + 3 = \square + 5$ d $7 \times 2 = 2 \times \square$

Write the number sentence. For the missing part, use a box ($\square$). Solve each number sentence.

46. The sum of five plus two is what number? ________

The sum of five and two is ________.

NAME ______________________ DATE ____________

Scoring Record for Posttests, Mid-Test, and Final Test

		Performance			
Chapter Posttest	Your Score	Excellent	Very Good	Fair	Needs Improvement
1	____ of 54	51–54	44–50	33–43	32 or fewer
2	____ of 43	41–43	35–40	27–34	26 or fewer
3	____ of 54	51–54	44–50	33–43	32 or fewer
4	____ of 45	43–45	37–42	28–36	27 or fewer
5	____ of 59	56–59	48–55	36–47	35 or fewer
6	____ of 51	48–51	42–47	32–41	31 or fewer
7	____ of 24	23–24	20–22	16–19	15 or fewer
8	____ of 15	15	13–14	10–12	9 or fewer
9	____ of 34	33–34	28–32	21–27	20 or fewer
10	____ of 46	44–46	38–43	29–37	28 or fewer
11	____ of 25	24–25	21–23	16–20	15 or fewer
12	____ of 52	49–52	43–48	32–42	31 or fewer
13	____ of 63	60–63	51–59	39–50	38 or fewer
Mid-Test	____ of 121	114–121	98–113	74–97	73 or fewer
Final Test	____ of 155	145–155	125–144	94–124	93 or fewer

Record your test score in the Your Score column. See where your score falls in the Performance columns. Your score is based on the total number of required responses. If your score is fair or needs improvement, review the chapter material.

I wish to ha

a air ,

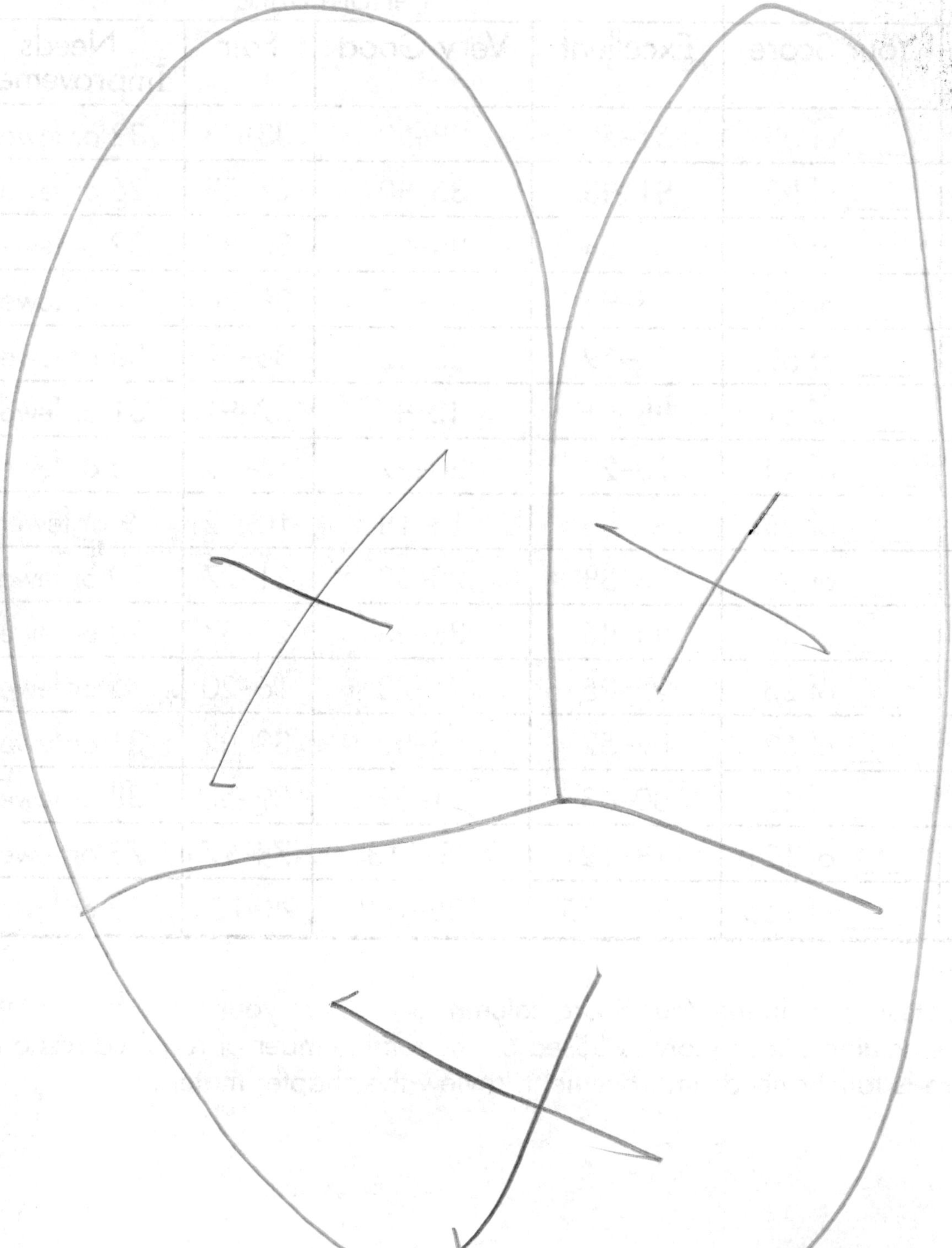